Praise
Reality By...

While you won't see Winona Ryder's name on the cover of this book, you will find some star power in it—the power to create star learners in our classrooms using cutting-edge tools! *Reality Bytes* will you give you the tools, the pedagogy, and a practical framework to bring the new reality of learning into your classroom.

Kasey Bell
Author of *Shake Up Learning:*
Practical Ideas to Move Learning from Static to Dynamic
@shakeuplearning

Creating engaging lessons that successfully integrate technology can be challenging. The team at Ready Learner One is here to help with their new book, *Reality Bytes*. In this book, you will find tons of images, classroom stories, and ideas that will help you create student-centered lessons. *Reality Bytes* includes ready-to-use lessons that will allow your students to experience content in a whole new way. No matter the grade level, there is something for everyone in this wonderfully immersive book.

Alice Keeler
Teacher, edtech expert, Google Certified Innovator
@alicekeeler

The Ready Learner One team provides a comprehensive look at VR and AR in *Reality Bytes*. They explain, showcase, and provide great examples of how these technologies can be used in the classroom. But, more importantly, the team has developed a workable, practical framework so any educator can easily scaffold their own use of these technologies to support teaching and learning. With the included background history, standards-based connections, and the emphasis on preparing students for their futures, this book is a must-read!

Kathy Schrock
Educational technologist
@kathyschrock

The Ready Learner One team has painted a clear picture of how augmented and virtual reality can transform the learning experience through the pages of *Reality Bytes*. Woven with stories from educators, hands-on learning experiences, and a framework that defines the various styles of adoption, *Reality Bytes* is as much an engaging read as it is a guide to developing engaging learning.

Thomas C. Murray
Director of innovation, Future Ready Schools
@thomascmurray

The Ready Learner One team clearly understands the need for a practical approach to learning. Their work emphasizes the value of helping students to not only absorb and blend content but also to create and to express themselves in bold new ways.

Sylvia Duckworth
Author of *How to Sketchnote:*
A Step-by-Step Manual for Teachers and Students
@sylviaduckworth

Reality Bytes is a must-have guidebook for the purposeful use of emergent technologies in the classroom. It lays out a plan for how educators can powerfully infuse these new tools into their classrooms! The authors offer a well-designed and easy-to-understand framework through which pedagogy drives the adoption of both AR and VR, allowing for meaningful learning experiences. From my favorite 90s movie to my now favorite AR/VR book—*Reality Bytes* should be read by educators everywhere!

Holly Clark
Author of *The Google Infused Classroom*
@HollyClarkEdu

One of the greatest challenges in using emerging technologies in education is the creative translation of technical capacities into meaningful and practical pedagogical solutions. *Reality Bytes* helps teachers address this challenge with brilliant examples of how AR and VR can become powerful tools to enhance learning experiences.

Yong Zhao
Foundation Distinguished Professor, University of Kansas,
and author of *Never Send a Human to Do a Machine's Job:*
Correcting the Top 5 Ed Tech Mistakes
@YongZhaoEd

Reality Bytes opens the doors to tools for meeting every student no matter where they are. This book outlines the power that AR and VR have in building empathy and growing critical worldviews and perspectives. Christine, Jesse, and Micah cast an exciting vision for the future of education!

Ken Shelton
Educational strategist, equity and inclusion consultant
@k_shelton

Reality Bytes will be one of the most important resources you need to launch confidently into the forefront of new and emerging technologies. While this interactive book will pique your curiosity with examples ranging from current classroom lessons to pop culture to build your understanding of augmented reality and virtual reality, it will also guide you through researched frameworks for instruction and learning that enable you to get started right away. *Reality Bytes* is a powerful, must-read book for those who wish to integrate technology into authentic learning experiences.

Lisa Highfill
Author of *The Hyperdocs Handbook*
@lisahighfill

Preparing awesome learning moments is so important for teachers because those moments can lead to powerful, meaningful learning opportunities that inspire curiosity and passion in our students. *Reality Bytes* shows us how to use emergent tools to spark enthusiasm and engagement in our classes by delivering artifacts to our students and transporting them to amazing places. I am thankful to have the Ready Learner One team as part of my PLN tribe!

Trevor MacKenzie
Author of *Dive into Inquiry* and *The Inquiry Mindset*
@trev_mackenzie

Jesse, Christine, and Micah have authored a powerful and practical book that brings AR and VR into the classroom. Their work takes a level-up approach to your existing lessons and infuses them with the 4 Cs and the ISTE standards in engaging and empowering ways.

Michael Cohen, the Tech Rabbi
Author of *Educated by Design*
@TheTechRabbi

Some experiences leave you wondering if you've been in a cave watching shadows. As a thirty-year teacher, school leader, and educational consultant, I've had plenty of great moments in the realm of teaching and learning. However, the number of times I feel I've stepped into that top-most tier can be counted on one hand, and the first time I put on a VR headset was certainly one of them.

In *Reality Bytes*, Christine Lion-Bailey, Jesse Lubinsky, and Micah Shippee have worked to bring the transformative potential of AR and VR in education into a framework of stories that speak to both the philosophical and practical needs for anyone wanting to understand the power of XR (extended reality). The book is a launchpad to experiencing something more, and any educator looking for tools that will grab the attention of their students in powerful ways would benefit from engaging with its stories and resources.

Rushton Hurley
Executive director, Next Vista for Learning
@rushtonh

I'm convinced that VR and AR are going to transform the classroom of the future by deepening empathy and expanding engagement, but only if thoughtful teachers get beyond the gee-whiz factor of introducing a new gadget. Look no further than *Reality Bytes* to guide you through a meaningful and authentic method to truly improve learning with this breakthrough technology.

Kevin Brookhouser
Author of *The 20time Project* and *Code in Every Class*
@brookhouser

Whether you are brand new to augmented and virtual reality or have extensive experience, this book will help you gain tremendous insight into integrating these technologies into your classroom. Christine, Jesse, and Micah have created an outstanding resource in the XR ABC framework, and they've highlighted each segment with engaging classroom stories and ideas. This book is a must-have for any teacher wanting to know more about AR and VR in the classroom.

Mari Venturino
Middle school science teacher
@mariventurino

As a classroom teacher who is always searching out new and innovative practices, I found the validation and support my pedagogy needed in *Reality Bytes*. The Ready Learner One team has created a well-researched and nicely put-together guidebook that answers the question of what's next in the classroom. Nicely done, y'all.

Donnie Piercey
Fifth grade teacher
@mrpiercEy

For both the teacher who has no clue what XR is and the tech-savvy teacher who is familiar with the concepts explored, *Reality Bytes* is the perfect addition to every educator's library. Through examples and stories from practicing educators, this book offers readers a clear understanding of new XR phenomena and a concise roadmap for how to effectively integrate XR into the classroom.

Jeffery Heil
Classroom teacher and edtech consultant
@jheil65

AR and VR's potential in the classroom is staggering! *Reality Bytes* is a candid, clever, and indispensable resource for any educator interested in navigating these emerging technologies. Even the book itself models how purposeful pedagogy and technology can intertwine!

Jessica L. Williams
Technology integration specialist
@jlenore24

Finally! Christine, Jesse, and Micah have created a phenomenal resource chock-full of practical how-to tips for absorb, blend, and create AR and VR experiences in K–12 education! *Reality Bytes* removes the fear sometimes associated with the words "augmented and virtual reality." Readers walk away with real-life examples and explanations of the power of AR and VR, ready and equipped to change the lives of the students they interact with every day!

Natasha Rachell
Digital learning specialist, Atlanta Public Schools
@apsitnatasha

REALITY
BYTES

REALITY
BYTES

INNOVATIVE LEARNING USING AUGMENTED AND VIRTUAL REALITY

CHRISTINE LION-BAILEY
JESSE LUBINSKY
MICAH SHIPPEE, PHD

DAVE BURGESS
Consulting, Inc.

Reality Bytes: Innovative Learning Using Augmented and Virtual Reality

© Christine Lion-Bailey, Jesse Lubinsky, Micah Shippee, PhD

This book is available at special discounts when purchased in quantity for use as premiums, promotions, fundraisers, or educational purposes. For inquiries and details, contact the publisher at books@daveburgessconsulting.com.

Published by Dave Burgess Consulting, Inc.
San Diego, CA
DaveBurgessConsulting.com
Library of Congress Control Number: 2019950629
Paperback ISBN: 978-1-949595-91-8
Ebook ISBN: 978-1-949595-92-5

Cover design by Chad W. Beckerman
Interior design by Kevin Callahan/BNGO Books

For Lilia and Jack: You are the absolute light of my life, and I love you more than you will ever know. Thank you for being my inspiration, showing me unconditional love, and teaching me to be a mom. For Mike: Thank you for always believing in me, your patience, and your support. I could have never done this without you, and I love you. For my parents and sister: For being the foundation upon which I have grown into the woman I am today—thank you. I love you.

CHRISTINE

For Jordan, Jackson, and Josie: Thank you for being the best teachers I've ever had. I learn more and more about what it means to be a good person from each of you every single day. My love and pride are boundless. For Jessica: I love you. Thank you for being the rock of the family and an incredibly selfless partner. I'm continuously humbled by your compassion, support, and love. For Mom: Thank you for everything. None of this would have been possible without your support, and I am so grateful to be your son. Love you!

JESSE

For Laura, Bekah, Tripp, and Liberty: I love you. Thank you for giving up so much of our time together as we worked on this project. Watching your aha moments as we played with emergent technology inspired me to dive deeper and share with others.

MICAH

Contents

Foreword

Monica Arés,
Innovative Technology for Education,
Facebook Inc.

Education is on the cusp of a technology revolution right now: an interactive, experience-based approach is transforming the way we teach, learn, work, and play.

If someone had told me at the start of my career that I would be working at a major tech company on the development, integration, and advancement of immersive technology for education, I never would have believed them. First of all, the technology didn't even exist back then, and secondly, I was happy in my work as an actuary — or so I thought.

After spending three years creating mathematical models for insurance companies, I was asked to participate in a corporate outreach program that invited professionals to speak to students at public schools. I had always enjoyed being a student, so I was excited to see what it was like on the other side of the classroom. The opportunity for an afternoon away from my cubicle was also welcome.

I loved speaking and interacting with the students, but I found out quickly how little teaching and learning was actually taking place in the schools I was visiting. Thinking back to what got me excited about learning, I landed on a series of memories from college. I remembered using technology in the classroom and being able to model the orbits of planets and the topography of mountains or find repeated patterns throughout nature like spirals in flowers, fingerprints, and galaxies. The technology made the material come alive, and I was hooked. Why, I started to wonder, weren't we bringing these methods of teaching to students at the high-school and middle-school levels?

It became clear to me that I wanted to be part of solving that problem. Against well-meaning advice, I left my job as an actuary at Deloitte to become a full-time graduate student focused on developing curricula using new technology. With my degree in hand, I put my skills to the test by becoming an educator for the next ten years. It is worth mentioning that as a teacher I was terrified every single day. Not of teaching — I loved that part—but of not keeping my students engaged. My goal was never to turn them into mathematicians or astronomers but to make them feel the rush of curiosity, a feeling that I knew could propel them to become lifelong learners. Curiosity motivates you to learn on your own, to think deeper, and to question the way things have always been done in hopes of finding new solutions. I believe it is the first and most necessary step to innovation.

Over the course of my teaching years, I noticed two unexpected trends. The first was that the best inventors, brainstormers, and problem solvers were seven-year-olds; they questioned everything, noticed new things, lived in wonder, and challenged the function and purpose of everything around them. The second was that students seemed markedly less curious starting in their middle-school years. The seven-year-olds had taught me that we are all hardwired to want to learn, so to see that curiosity die off just a few years later was troubling.

Students can begin to wonder after seeing astonishing feats and extraordinary talents, learning about scientific discoveries that push boundaries, or even getting a simple invitation to think about the unknown. Often, just engaging with the world around them leads to curiosity. But it is not always easy to experience the world when you are sitting in a classroom, especially when teaching materials are outdated. As an educator, I spent long nights trying to create lessons that were immersive, visually rich, and connected the real world to the material, but the resources I had to work with, including strictly 2-D surfaces, limited my creativity.

In my second week of working at Facebook, I was given an Oculus demonstration. The moment I put the headset on, I knew that it was the perfect medium for the kinds of lessons I'd been trying to create. I was also overcome by the feeling that I was witnessing a rare occurrence in education—the moment when technology comes along and shakes things up.

Although our generation built this technology, it is the next generation that will make it great, which means that part of our responsibility is to continue to pave the path forward. We have to understand that pushing the boundaries of new technology and making it accessible requires trial and error, persistence, creativity and a whole lot of grit. We don't just want students learning with AR/VR, we want them creating with it for generations to come.

Immersive technologies are just starting out, and many people are reluctant to adopt them because development is still unfolding. The things we criticize today, however, will be improved by the next wave of new hires. And those new hires are currently sitting in our classrooms. I love Marc Prensky's idea that we are digital immigrants, and our students are digital natives.

They are the ones who are fluent in the language of technology and understand the landscape and capabilities better than we ever could. Supporting our students, however, means that teachers and professors will need to step into our own curiosity and take on the roles of creators, explorers, designers, innovators, and mentors to encourage invention.

XR is changing how we teach, create, and learn. This book leads you on an excellent journey through the ways in which virtual and augmented reality have the power to revolutionize the content we consume, how we connect with others around the globe, and our ability to become creators of interactive 3-D worlds and models. I am thrilled that you will be taking that journey into the world of immersive technologies and the changing landscape of education.

Introduction

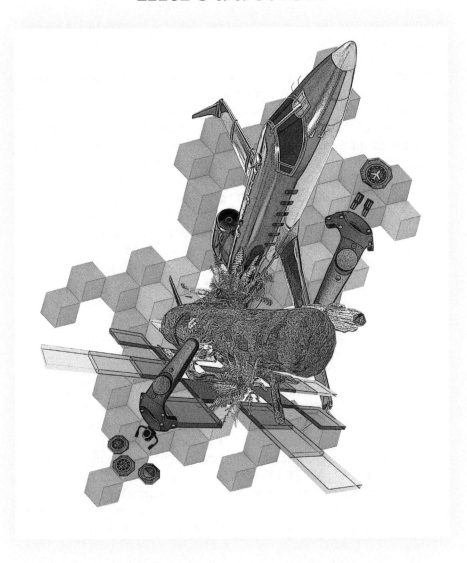

Maybe you're an educator who's heard about all this VR and AR stuff, and you want to learn more. Or maybe you're someone who has a good deal of experience with these technologies, and you just want to see how other educators are using them and what's new in the field. Perhaps you're a total technophobe and you're not really sure exactly what augmented and virtual reality are and how they play a role in education. Whatever the reason you picked up this book, our intention is to provide you with a clear understanding of augmented and virtual reality as well as some examples of how these technologies can be used to transform teaching and learning—examples that you can apply in your life right now!

Why virtual and augmented reality? These aren't just new technologies that improve what we are already doing in our classrooms: they provide us with ways to completely reinvent and recontextualize the experiences we design for our students. These technologies are not brand new (as you'll see throughout the book, examples of them have been popping up in film and television for years), but they haven't been widely adopted in education yet. There are a few reasons for that—the cost of devices, issues with mobility and ease of use in practice, and developers' lack of awareness of the need for educational-space content—but those challenges have been dwindling. More and more innovative educators have been finding ways to build these technologies into their instructional designs.

Our goal is for you to join them feeling excited, emboldened, and empowered: excited by the possibilities that these technologies offer; emboldened by the stories of educators just like you who are already using them to create meaningful change in schools; and empowered through the support and resources this text offers to help get you on your way.

While both virtual reality and augmented reality require various devices to make them work, throughout this text we've provided you with a variety of hands-on experiences that you can leverage using the technology you're probably closest to right now—your phone. And we know that any new education technology should always center on teaching and learning. With that in mind, we've developed a framework to help you place each type of learning experience into an educational context and compare it to other learning and standards that may already be a part of your vernacular. We call it the XR ABC framework. XR stands for "extended reality," and ABC stands for "Absorb, Blend, Create." (More on these terms in the next chapter.)

But before we jump into how educators like you are using these amazing technologies to change the face of teaching and learning, let's travel back in time to find out how we got here.

What is VR and AR?

So what are we talking about when we say virtual reality (VR) and augmented reality (AR)? Many assume that AR and VR are pretty similar, but they are, in fact, quite different technologies, particularly in how they relate to the physical world around us. Whether you've ever played a game like Pokémon Go! on your smartphone, watched a football game on TV where the first down line appears magically over the field, used Snapchat filters, or viewed the world through Google Cardboard, chances are good that you've already experienced AR and VR in your everyday life.

The Augmented Reality for Enterprise Alliance (AREA), the only global member-driven trade organization focused on reducing barriers to and accelerating the smooth introduction and widespread adoption of augmented reality by and for professionals, describes virtual reality as "technology that relies on software, hardware, and content but without the physical world and is 100% imaginary or synthetic." They define augmented reality, on the other hand, as technology that always involves adding digital information to someone's perception in a manner that's tightly synchronized with the physical world.[1]

We can think of augmented reality as both a suite of enabling technologies and the resulting experience of a user when highly contextual digital information (in the form of text, images, graphics, animations, video, 3-D models, sound, or haptic stimuli) is presented in a manner that's synchronized in real time and appears attached to physical-world people, places, or objects. Virtual reality, on the other hand, is an experience where users engage in an environment that is wholly imagined and rendered in digital form. As we dive into the world of AR and VR, it's very important to understand how these two distinct mediums for learning differ. Virtual reality is meant to take you somewhere else; augmented reality is meant to add to where you are.

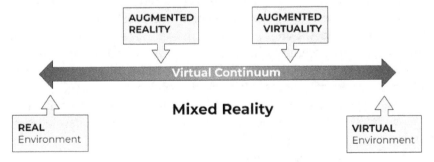

Mixed-Reality Continuum

We use the term "extended reality" (XR) to describe all AR, VR, and mixed-reality technologies on the XR spectrum.[2] A pure VR environment sits at one end of the spectrum, far removed from the physical world; on the other end of the spectrum, closer to our real-world environment, is augmented reality. "Mixed reality" (MR) can refer to any merging of real and virtual worlds to produce new environments and visualizations where physical and digital objects coexist and interact in real time, but sometimes the term MR can signify the middle of the XR spectrum: an enhanced version of AR where digitally rendered objects blend seamlessly into the environment and can be interacted with in a purposeful and thoughtfully designed way.

All types of XR can be leveraged to provide students with in-the-moment experiences that relate to their immediate surroundings. With XR we can deploy interactive museum pieces and models and transport students to locations relevant to their studies. We can also support student identification of elements and objects around them and throughout the world. These learning opportunities allow students to maintain an unprecedented sense of mindfulness. That is, through effective and efficient deployment of XR, students can achieve incresead levels of learning-centered awareness, making meaning at a whole new level. For instance, when studying anatomy, medical students are now able to use 3-D images in MR that allow them to manipulate, dissect, and examine parts of the human body without having to work on embalmed cadavers. And with that type of powerful technology available to them, you can see why they'd be "dead set" on using it! (Sorry, we had to.)

VR and AR in Education

Augmented and virtual reality have different strengths when it comes to instructional practice. Let's take a deep dive into some other researcher's definitions of VR and AR: VR is notable for its capacity to create "interactive computer-generated worlds, which substitute real-world sensory perceptions for digitally generated ones, producing the sensation of actually being in life-size new environments."[2] The most significant advantage of AR is its unique capacity to create immersive hybrid-learning environments that combine digital and physical objects, thereby facilitating the development of processing skills such as critical thinking, problem solving, and communicating through interdependent collaborative exercises.[3] These definitions clearly show that AR and VR are, indeed, two different mediums for learning.

Another difference is the way that augmented and virtual reality are experienced. For example, VR can be experienced through a head-mounted device that blocks out the real world (examples include Google Cardboard, Oculus, and the HTC Vive). But it can also be experienced on a laptop or tablet screen.

Likewise, AR experiences come in several forms.

- Target-based AR uses your device's camera to trigger a response from something such as a QR code.
- Location-based AR uses GPS coordinates and other geolocation features sometimes connected to Wi-Fi to launch an AR experience for the user. This is not dependent on a specific target but rather on the location of the device being used.
- Device-based AR requires downloading a particular application to view AR in the real world. Think of the filters you can add to your face when you take a selfie.

We are starting to see the application of these emergent technologies in many different fields: industry, medicine, business, higher education, and now K–12. The uses for AR and VR are rapidly expanding, and they are among the few technologies that we can most definitely target as relevant to our students' future workplaces. Our students will be called upon to leverage these technologies and to improve them in their careers. It's been predicted that by 2025 fourteen million workers will use AR in their workplace, up from four hundred thousand at present.[4]

So what can we do in the classroom? We need to share our experiences with AR and VR in order to better inform the creators of educational applications when they develop student-learning experiences. Researchers say, "While AR technology has been improving, it can still be difficult for students to use; therefore, more studies related to the development and usability of AR applications are needed. Within this line, learners' opinions about usability and preferences must be examined in AR based learning environments."[5] "Studies," in this case, should include information from our classroom experiences as a form of action research to promote meaningful change in the practice and use of innovative technology.

While it's easy to get wrapped up in the excitement and enthusiasm students have around trying something new, we need to recognize AR and VR as tools by which our students can increase understanding and achieve learning objectives. The most powerful learning experiences are created in the conversation that follows the tool's use. With that in mind, in the next chapter we will begin our journey by sharing the XR ABC framework, which we've developed to help you understand how VR and AR can be used to improve teachers' instructional practices and students' learning outcomes. It defines the ways that both AR and VR can be adopted in the learning environment. The importance of this kind of framework is that even as the tools change and become even more advanced over time, it ensures that the way we integrate them into our schools continues to be applicable.

How We've Designed This Book

The XR in XR ABC framework indicates that the framework addresses both AR and VR, and the ABC refers to the three styles of adopting these technologies: Absorb, Blend, and Create. The next chapter will further define each of these styles.

The six chapters after that are dedicated to the six aspects of the framework. Each of these six framework chapters contain the following components:

- *Beyond the Classroom:* A brief intro story from one of us about how this technology has impacted us in the real world.
- *Getting Started:* A hands-on activity that will allow you to begin experiencing the technology we discuss in the chapter.
- *Pop-Culture Connections:* Answering the question "Where have I seen this before?" Examples of AR and VR ideas put to use in your favorite movies and shows.
- *Classroom Chronicles:* Stories from practicing educators about how they've utilized this aspect of the framework. Each of these is followed by two components:
  - *Leveling Up in the Classroom:* Providing context for each story and helping you take the educator's idea and build it into classrooms at different grade levels and subject areas.

- o *XR ABC Toolbox:* Mapping each story out to show where it lands within common standards for STEM, twenty-first-century skills, and technology. The Toolbox also provides resources and links to free online content specific to each story to help you get started as you explore VR and AR technologies.
- *Where Do We Go from Here:* Providing a sense of where a particular piece of technology is going.
- *Join the Conversation:* Thinking questions that will encourage ongoing conversations on Twitter using our hashtag #ReadyLearnerOne.

Following the framework chapters, we'll hear from someone involved in creating these VR and AR educational experiences for our students, Lorenzo Vallone, a developer and the cofounder of Xennial Digital. How does someone in his role view these technologies? What goes into developing them for education? Here, we take a deep dive into how we can help create more meaningful experiences to impact education.

Throughout the book, you will see QR codes like the one below, which will take you to our company website. Some of these QR codes, like those at the start of each chapter and in the Getting Started sections, will take you to experiences for you to enjoy that will ground you in the ideas presented in each chapter. Others, like the ones in the XR ABC Toolbox for each story, will bring you to resources to help supplement your learning. In either case, we recommend you use them to help enhance your experience of *Reality Bytes*.

1

The XR ABC Framework

The Introduction of XR into Education

Education is changing because the world is changing. As new tools become more accessible and their potential is better understood by educators, we will see instructional shifts that benefit our students. How quickly these shifts happen is directly correlated to how much access educators have to research-based, best practice-tested guidance. The XR ABC framework at the heart of this book is exactly that kind of guidance, and we've developed it with the hope that it can accelerate adoption of XR technologies. Like the framework, that hope is grounded in research: we've seen the effects that good guidance can have in speeding the adoption and benefits of technology in research.

New research is showing us that XR learning experiences really are making a difference. The University of Maryland conducted one of the first in-depth analyses on whether people learn better through immersive virtual environments. The researchers split participants (largely unfamiliar with VR) into two groups: one viewed information first via a VR head-mounted display and then on a desktop; the other did the opposite. The results showed an 8.8 percent overall improvement in recall accuracy for participants using VR headsets, a statistically significant number according to the research team.[1] We have no doubt that more of this kind of research will continue to support what many of us already know: XR has a positive future in education.

The rate at which we adopt emergent technology to achieve our instructional goals is important; it affects how we can best prepare our students for their futures. Sometimes we need to pause to truly understand our goals and objectives for leveraging emergent technology. Before we move forward and explore XR's potential, we must understand that education and technology have had a long partnership. From that partnership, we can learn lessons that will benefit us all as we move forward with XR. One of the clearest examples of emergent technology's influence on education can be seen in the history of radio—high technology in the nineteenth and early twentieth centuries.

Historical Innovation in Education

In 1895, Guglielmo Marconi carried out the first experimental transmission of wireless signals, first over a distance of four hundred and then at two thousand meters.[2] Twenty-five years later the instructional uses of radio technology began to develop, and radio as a medium for distance learning began to be explored. That's right—there was a twenty-five-year gap between the development of the technology and exploration into its instructional uses. Today we want to get going with the latest and greatest as soon as possible.

Historically, cultural forces have contributed to an educational perspective that embraces newer, trending technology, specifically in regard to film, radio, television, and eventually computers. In the 1920s, parents and businesses supplied schools across the United States with radio receivers in an effort to integrate trending technology into their children's educational experiences. They understood that providing students with access to emergent technology in an educational setting would help prepare children for their futures.

However, the adoption of radio in education was delayed due to barriers that may be familiar to you even today, starting with poor battery life and poor reception. Additionally, educators were unsure about how radio technology could be used to improve learning and learning outcomes. Imagine classroom closets full of unused radios. Radio's history in the classroom reminds us that technology, while very important, does not by itself equate to actual instructional value.

But even with these barriers in place, momentum gained around radio technology. In the 1930s, industry and educational leaders predicted film and radio would be great catalysts of a revolutionary shift in instructional delivery. In 1932 Benjamin Darrow, founder of the Ohio School of the Air, said, "The central and dominant aim of education by radio is to bring the world to the classroom, to make universally available the services of the finest teachers, the inspiration of the greatest leaders ... and unfolding events which through the radio may come as a vibrant and challenging textbook of the air."[3] Radio, it seemed, was going to cause a shift in the instructional paradigm.

In 1947 the invention of the transistor, a tiny semiconductor device, led to the introduction of a new kind of radio that used dry cells rather than vacuum tubes. This meant they consumed much less power and were more reliable, less expensive, lighter, and smaller than their predecessors.[4]

Following the pattern of Moore's law — which predicts that over time technologies get more accessible as they increase in capability — radios would continue to become smaller, more powerful, and more user-friendly. By the end of the 1970s, 70 percent of radio receivers were either portable or mobile;[5] better battery life and reception followed. Educational institutions needed to answer a new question: how can radio be used to improve learning and learning outcomes?

Educators hoping to use radio broadcasts for instruction often had no control over the content. These ground-level decision-makers were hesitant to integrate the technology in their particular educational contexts because of the lack of control over content delivery. But over time, as scheduling and broadcast regulation grew, radio became more frequently used for instructional delivery.[6]

The challenge left to overcome now was the technology's primary issue: in its original form, radio was a one-way communication medium. Interaction with listeners was minimal. As a result, a radio program's pace was set by the broadcaster, who found it difficult to gauge the listener's prior knowledge and attitudes, which are critical to learning.[7] To develop instructional value when using radio to replace teacher lectures, instructors began to include preparatory and follow-up materials. These materials were packaged with visual and print materials and interactive elements that could be organized via listening groups.[8] The relationship between radio and instructional material became symbiotic: as materials to work with radio for instructional purposes became more effective, so too did radio broadcasts. Methodology was developed to combine radio broadcasts with teacher instruction to facilitate a deferred-response dialogue with a roomful of students.[9] (A similar strategy is applied today when Dora the Explorer pauses after asking a question, hoping the viewer is responding.)

Radio technology has been deployed throughout the last century to reach geographically dispersed groups in need of cost-effective educational support, and by 2001, radio had become the most important medium for communication and social change worldwide.[10] The saying "knowledge is power" is commonly attributed to Sir Francis Bacon, and it seems particularly relevant to understanding the impact radio technology had on the world. Radio allowed thought and insights to spread around the globe, and social change followed, much like the way the printing press led to increased literacy, which led to the flourishing of critical thinking.

The many affordances of radio in education technology did not come without difficulty. For most emergent technologies, barriers centered on accessibility often cause the primary delays for widespread adoption in education. Like radio, XR technologies will be used for instruction, but when? Will it take one hundred years for XR to reach its potential? With time, costs will go down and access will go up. But access is not enough to bring about the paradigm shifts necessary to change education for the better.

Shifting the Paradigm for XR Adoption

A 2002 comprehensive review of research compared traditional classroom-based instruction to technology-supported instruction and found no significant benefit from adding technology to instruction.[11] This might seem counterintuitive to our arguments for the educational benefits of XR, but a deeper dive into the research reveals important, productive insights. The authors of the review point to findings that state that the particular technology used in classrooms is not as important as other instructional factors, such as pedagogy and course design,[12] a point supported by past researchers who have identified that learning is affected more by what is delivered than by the delivery medium.[13] So we know that good teaching comes first. Our work here is to better understand and support emergent technologies (the medium) to improve learning and learning outcomes when we use technology to amplify good teaching practices.

As the examples of radio and other advances show, the most significant influence in the evolution of instructional-technology paradigm shifts is not always the technical development of more powerful devices but rather educators' understanding of how these technologies can be used to improve learning and learning outcomes.[14] It is in the adoption rather than integration of emergent technologies that we will start to see a meaningful shift in practice. After all, the word "adoption" conveys agency and choice, whereas "integration" connotes coercion without choice. Simply integrating new technology will not change our practices. It's adopting a positive approach to innovation that will lead to a paradigm shift to better meet the needs of students in the future.

To help educators adopt new technologies like XR, we need a way to describe research-based, best practice-tested applications. The XR ABC framework is a guide for focusing our conversations around effective and efficient uses of XR in education. The XR ABC framework provides a common language for instructional practice around XR while comprehensively illustrating objectives and standards, which can be used to communicate the effectiveness of instruction. The XR ABC framework has evolved from both research and best practices that demonstrate how XR can be used to improve learning and learning outcomes.

The XR ABC Framework

With XR, as well as other classroom software solutions, we often talk about consuming and creating as two levels of interactivity afforded by the technology, but through research and practice, we have found that an area exists between these two levels that is a combination, or blend, of capabilities. That's why the XR ABC framework describes three areas of interactivity in XR: Absorb, Blend, and Create.

Absorb experiences use readily available apps and experiences to engage students in things like virtual field trips and observations of 3-D models. These experiences support increased understanding and recall.

- In AR Absorb experiences, users observe content that augments or improves the learning experience with minimal interactivity. Absorbing with AR means using the technology to add to experiences in a relatively simple and static manner compared to Blending or Creating, where we are manipulating or building objects in AR. Absorb experiences are triggered by AR targets, geographic locations, or device-based apps. The applications of AR Absorb are WYSIWYG (what you see is what you get).

The learning curve is low for AR Absorb, and almost every student and educator can take advantage of the benefits it offers right away.
- Virtual reality Absorb experiences allow users to visit distant places and see new things from a first-person perspective. VR Absorb experiences are WYSIWYG with a low interactivity level. Simple VR Absorb field trips can be incredibly powerful when paired with meaningful conversations and thoughtful instructional delivery.

Blending means to modify existing content by employing available apps and experiences. Users in Blend experiences can manipulate (rather than create) objects, like characters, blocks, etc., that are preloaded into XR applications in order to apply, analyze, and evaluate content.

- In augmented reality, Blend learners have the opportunity to change the outcome of an experience while working within preexisting content. AR Blend goes a step beyond Absorb because manipulation and change are included in the experience. It is engaging for learners while still intuitive for those who are not ready for the concept of creation.
- VR Blend allows users to consume content while manipulating it. In VR, Blend affords learners the opportunity to change the immersive experience's outcome while working within preexisting content. VR Blend allows users the opportunity to have a choice in a more meaningful and personalized VR encounter.

In our framework, Creating means developing new content by leveraging available tools to synthesize and construct experiences. Create experiences are used to truly demonstrate an understanding of content through the construction of new XR experiences, objects, stories, etc.

- In augmented reality, Create learning experiences allow the learner to develop new content rather than simply consuming it. For learners to create their own content, educators must shift their mind-set regarding the learning process. For students to create these experiences themselves is learning at a much higher level.
- VR Create is a game changer for students since it allows them to use their own ideas and imaginations to demonstrate real learning and understanding. Students become owners of learning, architects of content, and developers of brave new worlds.

It is very important not to think about the XR ABC framework as levels of mastery that lead to Creating. Create should not be the only style used in our instructional practices. Each of the areas has potential to positively impact instruction when leveraged appropriately. For example, taking students on a simple virtual field trip (a VR Absorb experience) can be powerful when aligned with class-lesson objectives. Having the students create a fictional world is not always the most productive choice.

The various kinds of interactivity found in XR—both now and in the future—can magnify positive instructional experiences, but we need to be able to effectively describe what is happening with XR in our classrooms. The XR ABC framework's Absorb, Blend, and Create terminology gives us a common language we can use to dive deep in conversations about harnessing the power of these exciting new technologies.

The XR ABC Framework Toolbox

As a companion to the XR ABC framework, we have prepared a toolbox to illustrate how XR can be used to improve learning and learning outcomes.

XR ABC TOOLBOX

Area of Interactivity | Experience
Use Case
Tags: (Content and strategy types)

Platform: Devices or system requirements

Tool: Application information

Five Es (STEM)	Four Cs	ISTE Standards for Students
☐ Engage	☐ Communication	☐ Empowered Learner
☐ Explore	☐ Critical Thinking	☐ Digital Citizen
☐ Explain	☐ Creativity	☐ Knowledge Constructor
☐ Elaborate	☐ Collaboration	☐ Innovative Designer
☐ Evaluate		☐ Computational Thinker
		☐ Creative Communicator
		☐ Global Collaborator

ISTE Standards for Educators	SAMR	QR Code for Additional Resources
☐ Learner	☐ Substitution	
☐ Leader	☐ Augmentation	
☐ Citizen	☐ Modification	
☐ Collaborator	☐ Redefinition	
☐ Designer		
☐ Facilitator		
☐ Analyst		

Five Es (STEM)

The Five Es are STEM-based standards that consist of the following stages of learning: engaging, exploring, explaining, elaborating, and evaluating. These stages come from cognitive psychology, constructivist-learning theory, and best practices in teaching.[15]

Four Cs

The Four Cs originated in the "Framework for 21st Century Learning," which highlighted eighteen different skills. Eventually, the National Education Association (NEA) stated that "over the years it became clear that the framework was too long and complicated." To make the framework more user-friendly for educators, the NEA worked to identify which skills were most critical in K–12 education. The NEA found consensus in four specific skill areas, which became known as the Four Cs: critical thinking, communication, collaboration, and creativity.[16]

ISTE Standards for Students

The ISTE (International Society for Technology in Education) Standards for Students are designed to empower students' voices and ensure that learning is a student-driven process. Through the application of the ISTE Standards for Students, we can intentionally design learning experiences that focus on different roles for students as learners:

- **Empowered Learner:** Students leverage technology to take an active role in choosing, achieving, and demonstrating competency in their learning goals, informed by the learning sciences.
- **Digital Citizen:** Students recognize the rights, responsibilities, and opportunities of living, learning and working in an interconnected digital world, and they act and model in ways that are safe, legal, and ethical.
- **Knowledge Constructor:** Students critically curate a variety of resources using digital tools to construct knowledge, produce creative artifacts, and make meaningful learning experiences for themselves and others.
- **Innovative Designer:** Students use a variety of technologies within a design process to identify and solve problems by creating new, useful, or imaginative solutions.
- **Computational Thinker:** Students develop and employ strategies for understanding and solving problems in ways that leverage the power of technological methods to develop and test solutions.

- **Creative Communicator:** Students communicate clearly and express themselves creatively for a variety of purposes using the platforms, tools, styles, formats, and digital media appropriate to their goals.
- **Global Collaborator:** Students use digital tools to broaden their perspectives and enrich their learning by collaborating with others and working effectively in teams locally and globally.[17]

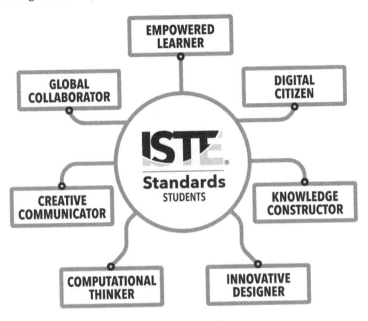

ISTE Standards for Educators

The ISTE Standards for Educators are meant to support educators in helping students become empowered learners. Through the application of the ISTE Standards for Educators, instructors can develop their different facets as educators:

- **Learner:** Educators continually improve their practice by learning from and with others and exploring proven and promising practices that leverage technology to improve student learning.
- **Leader:** Educators seek out opportunities for leadership to support student empowerment and success and to improve teaching and learning.
- **Citizen:** Educators inspire students to positively contribute to and responsibly participate in the digital world.
- **Collaborator:** Educators dedicate time to collaborate with both colleagues and students to improve practice, discover and share resources and ideas, and solve problems.

- **Designer:** Educators design authentic, learner-driven activities and environments that recognize and accommodate learner variability.
- **Facilitator:** Educators facilitate learning with technology to support student achievement of the ISTE Standards for Students.
- **Analyst:** Educators understand and use data to drive their instruction and support students in achieving their learning goals.[18]

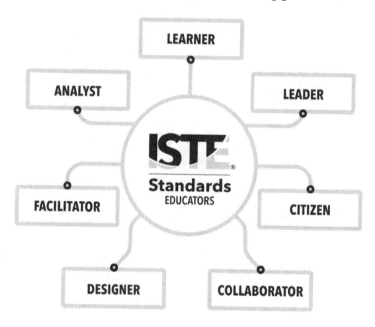

SAMR

One of the most powerful ways to frame discussions with colleagues regarding technology adoption and pedagogical-shift strategies is to refer to the SAMR (substitution, augmentation, modification, redefinition) model.[19] This model calls for substituting an existing strategy for one supported by emergent technology. We then augment the strategy when we find that technology can improve (rather than replace) it. Next, we use technology to modify the strategy. Finally, we may redefine the entire strategy when we find technology can offer us a better way of doing things. Simply put, the SAMR Model helps each of us to rethink individual lessons, units, and instructional practice.[20]

Conclusion

The XR ABC framework was developed for educators, who are undeniably the most important aspect of any learner's experience. Built with input from the voices of experienced educators and research-based, the framework provides a pathway for XR to be used to improve learning and learning outcomes while laying out a common language to guide our growth with the meaningful adoption of XR technologies in education.

2

AR Absorb

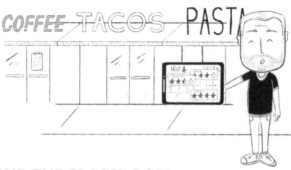

BEYOND THE CLASSROOM

Many of us come across a new technology while looking to solve a problem. Sometimes, the problem is small, like trying to take a measurement without a ruler handy (there's an app for that). Other times, it's a matter of convenience. Think about using navigation software: you might already know the directions you need, but the ability to find the best route based on current traffic conditions is convenient and helpful. Then there are those times when technology is used to solve an immediate and critical problem. My introduction to augmented reality was one of these times.

I was on the way to meet friends for dinner before going to see a Broadway show (*The Book of Mormon,* in case you were interested). We had made plans to eat at one of my favorite spots. I got there a few minutes early and, much to my dismay, it had shut down! Now, that might not sound like a big problem to you. There are plenty of restaurants in New York City, so what's the big deal? Well for me—like many of you, I'm sure—finding time to get out of the house for a nice relaxing evening with family and friends can be an ordeal! There's the planning, the babysitting, the expenses, etc. You can't just pick a random spot to eat. The whole night could hinge on that decision!

So, standing on the corner of Tenth Avenue, I pulled out my phone and opened Yelp. The options seemed endless. I started sweating. And then I noticed the icon on the bottom of the app for something called Monocle. I didn't know what it was, but I clicked on it. The app opened up my camera, and when I held up my phone, I noticed that all of the restaurants up and down the street now had the Yelp ratings hovering just above them. It felt like magic! Instead of doing all kinds of unending research, I could just look at a restaurant through my phone and instantly have access to all of the reviews for that spot. My evening was saved—and for just the first of many times, augmented reality proved to be a real game changer in my life!

—*Jesse*

Getting Started

Before we jump in, let's take a look at an AR experience. On your device, go to 8th.io/jini or use the QR code below.

If you're thinking about skipping ahead without doing this, don't. You won't want to miss the chance to throw cash at a robot. We're not joking.

Note: QR codes require you to use your device's camera. Simply open your camera and hold it over the code. You will be prompted to open the link in a web browser.

What is AR Absorb?

When you hop in your car and go for a drive to an unknown place, do you go to AAA and pick up a TripTik Travel Planner? Probably not. At least not a paper one. We'll bet you use Google Maps, Waze, or GPS. You might be surprised to think of it this way, but you are already augmenting your driving experience through the use of these GPS mapping programs.

It's true — augmented reality is already a major part of our world, and like many meaningful innovations, it has become part of our everyday lives without us really realizing it. Maybe we aren't quite at the point we've seen in the movies, but we are getting there. Let's go back to the example of using your GPS. What could the next step look like? Well, what if instead of looking at your GPS device or phone, you could simply see directions and key information in a heads-up display (HUD) on your windshield? This is where AR Absorb comes into play.[1]

With AR Absorb, added content with minimal interactivity augments or improves your experience. HUDs have already been a way for users to absorb AR for over eighty years. You may remember seeing them in the planes in the movie *Top Gun*, but German fighter pilots were using them in 1937 in the form of reflector sights in their planes.[2] Since then, military and video-game uses of HUDs have only grown. In more recent times, we've seen HUDs used in Google Glass and DAQRI's motorcycle helmet (to name just a few). Is

AR technology part of the future of work? We would argue that it is absolutely a clear next step for work flows, thus it is worth understanding and experiencing with our students.

In education, AR Absorb experiences involve using devices with cameras to view content-rich objects. Imagine holding the solar system in your hand or being able to walk around a huge dinosaur right in your classroom! Like all AR, these experiences can be launched by targets, locations, or apps. The learning curve is low for AR Absorb, and almost every student and educator can take advantage of the benefits they offer right away.

Pop-Culture Connection

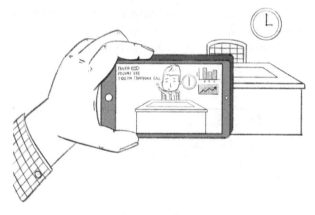

If you think you've seen this kind of technology before in a movie, you probably have. Think of Tony Stark getting information from Jarvis in his Iron Man suit, Robocop viewing the world through his helmet, or even the Predator looking to take out Arnold "The Governator" Schwarzenegger (whose Terminator movies are another good example of this technology). In one of our favorite recent examples, the film *Kingsman: The Golden Circle* shows what utilizing this technology for meetings could look like. The movie's AR-powered glasses are a great example of AR Absorb because besides displaying the images of the fellow meeting attendees, they provide no additional interaction between the user and the environment. Filmmakers and creative types have long imagined ways for AR technologies to be used in science fiction. But what seemed out of this world only a few years ago is quickly becoming commonplace and available to enhance the work we do in teaching and learning today.

CLASSROOM CHRONICLES
TRANSLATING THE WORLD
GEORGE BARCENAS

I was trying to read the sign for gates and times in the airport while rushing to catch a connecting flight. As I glanced up at the screen, I saw an older gentleman looking at the same panel. He was holding his phone up to the sign and reading it in his native language. At first, I was so impressed by the airport putting all these languages on its displays — then the reality of the situation hit me. There was only one language on the sign: we were both looking at the same words and reading them in two different languages.

Αεροδρομιο
Airport   14
Πειραιάς
Pireas   9

I stopped in my tracks and decided at that moment to miss my flight. What I had just witnessed was something I needed to know more about. I walked up to the gentleman and asked him what he was using to translate the signs with his phone. He just stared at me. Of course, the language barrier meant he didn't understand a word I said. I pointed at his phone and then to the screen. The old man responded to me in his native tongue. I was starting to say that I didn't understand when his phone spoke to me. His words were being translated into English as he spoke. We were able to hold a conversation using the phone as our translator. He showed me how his camera could instantly translate written words into his native language of Vietnamese.

When I asked him what app he was using to do this, I was expecting the name of an app that I had never heard of before. To my amazement, the app was Google Translate. While I was familiar with Google Translate as a tool in a browser, I was unaware of the magic that could be unlocked with it as an app on a mobile device. It allows users to interact with the world around them through the power of a phone or tablet's camera, microphone, and speakers.

This AR use of Google Translate provides new levels of access at the fingertips of those who previously would have been left without an adequate resource. For example, successfully completing job applications that feature endless intimidating paperwork when your native language isn't English is more easily achievable through the camera function of Google Translate.

This access greatly benefits both our students and their parents as we leverage technology to assist with breaking barriers. I have used the app to facilitate communication in parent-teacher conferences. It has been a life changer for families at our schools because of its ability to translate documentation in real time. Conversations are much more effective and authentic, and thus better relationships are being built. For students who struggle with homework and can't get help from their parents because of language barriers, the app has an even more assistive feature. The camera can scan a photo of a document; when a user highlights the words on the screen with a finger, the app reads them back in translation. I have had parents tell me that it not only has helped them understand their kids' homework but has also been a way for them to learn themselves. For some, literacy can pose a challenge even when words are translated, and the translation of words in both written and audio forms helps expand vocabularies. The Google Translate app has given our school families better access to the world around them.

I have always wondered what would've happened if I had just kept running to make my flight that day, how different my world would be because I didn't stop to learn. The experience has changed so many lives in the schools in our district. I believe that moments like this are meant to be.

LEVELING UP IN THE CLASSROOM

Google Translate is a powerful tool that can be used across classrooms of all grade levels and content areas. It is especially powerful for looking at imagery that connects to culture. For example, if you are exploring the concept of community in a lower elementary classroom, you can draw parallels to community buildings from other cultures. How about placing a photo of your local library next to one from Lyon, France? Have students use Google Translate to determine what the French building is by holding the device over the sign indicating the type of building. Once the French word "bibliothèque" translates to "library," students will label the picture of the building from their own community. To take this to the upper grade levels, use Google Translate to translate propaganda from historical eras such as World War II or the Cold War. The possibilities for connecting learning to global awareness and cultural studies via the power of Google Translate are endless. Happy translating!

XR ABC TOOLBOX

AR Absorb | Google Translate

Translating the World

Tags: world language, language arts, speaking, life skills

Platform: iOS and Android devices

Tools: Google Translate provides a service whereby writing can be translated into another language. This functions through the camera of the device. Additionally, there is the ability to have the word read to the user in the event that literacy is a challenge.

Five Es (STEM)	Four Cs	ISTE Standards for Students
√ **Engage**	√ **Communication**	☐ Empowered Learner
√ **Explore**	√ **Critical Thinking**	☐ Digital Citizen
☐ Explain	☐ Creativity	√ **Knowledge Constructor**
☐ Elaborate	√ **Collaboration**	☐ Innovative Designer
☐ Evaluate		☐ Computational Thinker
		√ **Creative Communicator**
		☐ Global Collaborator

ISTE Standards for Educators	SAMR	QR Code for Additional Resources
☐ Learner	☐ Substitution	
☐ Leader	√ **Augmentation**	
☐ Citizen	☐ Modification	
√ **Collaborator**	☐ Redefinition	
☐ Designer		
√ **Facilitator**		
☐ Analyst		

Κόσμος είναι στα χέρια σας!

Ready Learner Go!

If you don't have it already, add the Google Translate app to your phone or tablet. Open the camera function of the app and scan the text below for some Greek words of wisdom!

CLASSROOM CHRONICLES
ALL THE WORLD'S A STAGE
CHRISTINE LION-BAILEY

I have always prided myself on being a creative teacher. I work hard to think outside of the box and to bring curiosity and excitement to my classroom. Shakespeare wrote that "all the world's a stage," and I believe, with great conviction, that the classroom is the very first stage to which students are introduced. For teachers it is a stage designed to draw learners in through engagement and entertainment, and it is a stage for the students to show-case their learning and exude pride about their accomplishments. It is with this in mind that I seek to engage students in learning experiences that are rich with opportunities to demonstrate their learning in unique ways. Enter the MERGE Cube.

As a director of technology and innovation, it is my responsibility to guide teachers in innovative practices in their classrooms. While supporting teach-ers preparing to implement a sixth-grade science unit entitled "Earth's Place in the Universe," I wanted to find a way for the teacher to assess students' learning beyond the standard assessments. We typically perform assess-ments with traditional methods like multiple-choice and open-response tests, asking students to create models of the solar system, and assigning oral or slide presentations. While all of them got the job done, none of these methods are exciting, engaging, or innovative. The teacher and I were look-ing to take our assessments to the next level, and I wanted to incorporate innovative assessment strategies in the process. After chatting with a few

colleagues, I was introduced to the MERGE Cube. This handy little cube-shaped tool is made from hard foam, and it has the ability, through a variety of apps available on both mobile phones and tablets, to literally bring learning right into the hands of the students. By viewing the block through apps while holding and rotating it, students can explore and learn from a perspective never before possible.

With a MERGE Cube in my hands, an innovative assessment seemed much more attainable. Luckily, one of the apps available for the MERGE Cube is Galactic Explorer. Magic happened when students launched Galactic Explorer on their phones—yes, that is right, their phones; this is a perfect opportunity to embrace the BYOD (bring your own device) model and trust that the excitement of the lesson is enough to ensure students stay on task. Students simply pointed the cameras of their phones at the MERGE Cube. The app literally turned the cube in their hands into the solar system. As students turned the cube in their hands, the solar system rotated on the screen of their device. As they tapped on the various planets, the device zoomed in and showed the planet and anything relevant to it (moons, satellites, etc.). Students could access an information tab to gain more detailed information. Imagine being a middle-school student and literally holding the solar system in the palm of your hand!

Galactic Explorer and the MERGE Cube allowed our teachers to make their assessments on the solar system into the kind of innovative experience that I was yearning to provide for our students. We designed an assessment that required students to take viewers on a tour of the solar system. They needed to name the various celestial bodies in the solar system and provide three defining characteristics of each. Students utilized the MERGE Cube and Galactic Explorer to do this. There is a record feature in Galactic Explorer that students used to record their tours. Once their recordings were completed, students used the app Clips to add voiceovers and subtitles that named the planets and their defining characteristics. As a final step, students were required to upload their videos to YouTube to share with their peers.

The Galactic Explorer assessment project was engaging and innovative, and it sparked a curiosity in students not just to demonstrate their learning about the solar system but to explore augmented reality in new ways. After this assessment was completed, students began using the MERGE Cube for a variety of other explorations with various apps. Additionally, a group of students designed an oversized version of the MERGE Cube in an attempt to see how large of a solar system they could create inside of the classroom environment. Other students began to make their own MERGE Cube content through the CoSpaces MERGE Cube add-on. Regardless of their avenue of exploration, students' curiosity and desire to learn more were ignited by this AR assessment.

Interested in how this lesson works? Check out the XR ABC Toolbox for this story and scan the QR code for lesson plans and supporting information on preparing this lesson and adapting it for your classroom!

LEVELING UP IN THE CLASSROOM

So you love the idea of the MERGE Cube, but you just can't imagine how it connects to your classroom? Let us help! Galactic Explorer is just one of many apps that are compatible with the MERGE Cube. Are you an art teacher looking to explore ancient art with your students? How about if you could place the statue of the Ram of Amun directly into the palm of your students' hands, allowing them to explore the art from any angle? Try out the 3D Museum Viewer app. This incredible app not only allows you to hold the art for up-close study but also to explore works of art life-size in the classroom and record your process. There are tons of apps that inspire many interactive ways of engaging learners through the MERGE Cube. Using the MERGE Cube in your classroom literally brings learning into the hands of the students. It is kinesthetic in nature, provides a manipulative, and inspires creativity and critical thinking.

QUICK TIP

Have you ever felt challenged in your teaching by students' struggling to form context around historical events? If so, we've got great news! The British Broadcasting Company (BBC) offers an AR experience called Civilisations AR that allows us to bring artifacts right into the classroom. Civilisations AR provides full-scale 3-D models of over forty artifacts as AR experiences, from a Corinthian helmet dating to 550 BCE to the Clonmore shrine in County Armagh from the seventh century CE. The app allows learners to visualize the region of the world from which an artifact derives, read through important facts about its impact on human history, explore specific details about the artifact through a spotlight feature, and photograph the artifact in the learning environment. One fun extended use of Civilisations AR is to have students create a gallery backdrop in the classroom and then use the app to take photos of the artifacts in the classroom gallery.

AR Absorb | MERGE Cube—Galactic Explorer
All the World's a Stage
Tags: science, language arts, speaking

Platform: iOS and Android devices

Tools: The MERGE Cube is a soft black cube. QR-like designs painted in special reflective paint on its sides trigger AR experiences. A great advantage of the MERGE Cube is the accessibility of the AR experience.

MERGE Explorer uses innovative AR/VR spatial-learning technology to teach science topics from kindergarten through eighth grade in completely new ways. Students are able to visualize, hold, and interact with complex concepts using their own hands and the world around them for greater understanding, engagement, and achievement.

Five Es (STEM)
- √ **Engage**
- √ **Explore**
- ☐ Explain
- ☐ Elaborate
- ☐ Evaluate

Four Cs
- √ **Communication**
- ☐ Critical Thinking
- √ **Creativity**
- ☐ Collaboration

ISTE Standards for Students
- ☐ Empowered Learner
- ☐ Digital Citizen
- √ **Knowledge Constructor**
- √ **Innovative Designer**
- ☐ Computational Thinker
- ☐ Creative Communicator
- ☐ Global Collaborator

ISTE Standards for Educators
- ☐ Learner
- ☐ Leader
- ☐ Citizen
- ☐ Collaborator
- ☐ Designer
- √ **Facilitator**
- ☐ Analyst

SAMR
- ☐ Substitution
- √ **Augmentation**
- ☐ Modification
- ☐ Redefinition

QR Code for Additional Resources

Ready Learner Go!

Download the free MERGE Explorer app, open the Galactic Explorer experience, and hold your device over the picture to the left.

CLASSROOM CHRONICLES
UPGRADE THAT TEXTBOOK
DAVID SAUNDERS

The publishing world has been struggling to develop a textbook-distribution model that works well for schools. A quick survey of the catalog of digital textbooks shows that many titles are still not available. And when they are available, it's often difficult to manage student access with logins and purchase codes. As a result, some schools are hesitant to make a full transition to digital textbooks. This creates an enormous gap, as the primary mode of instruction remains years behind the student in whose hands the textbook resides!

The development of AR apps has presented an incredible opportunity to elevate the state of the textbook without completely pushing print textbooks aside. In short, augmented reality allows educators to easily create digital content that makes traditional textbooks more timely, informative, and engaging for students. Augmented textbooks provide the best of both analog and digital resources!

Not too long ago, I had the opportunity to work with one of our history teachers to augment a ninth-grade history textbook. Working together, we identified content areas that could be expanded and found digital resources to meet those needs.

Using an iPad and the iOS app Aurasma (now called HP Reveal), we built a series of interactive layers on top of the printed content. These layers led to digital resources meant to provide context, push understanding, and increase overall engagement and comprehension.

To create the hovering "learn more" buttons, I created a PNG image in Photoshop that I then imported as an image layer. Once it was added to the app as an Aura (interactive image), I added hyperlinks that led to webpages or videos for further reading or exploration.

We also created an augmented version of a biography of William Shakespeare written by Aliki. We tried to provide some historical context for the world of Shakespeare, and we used "learn more" buttons to lead readers toward exceptional examples of Shakespearean theater found on YouTube. We also experimented with adding a layer at the end of each chapter that would lead to a Google Form to collect student's reflections, questions, and understandings in order to better meet their needs.

LEVELING UP IN THE CLASSROOM

What are other ways a tool like HP Reveal (formerly Aurasma) allows learners opportunities to showcase their work? Imagine an open house evening at your school where the hallways are lined with student artwork. Every student, along with their parents, rushes down the hallway to their own piece of art where they provide a detailed account of the medium used, the subject of the artwork, and their perspective on the art. Now imagine walking down the same hallway and each piece of art is actually a trigger image: when accessed through the HP Reveal app, the artist appears and provides the same detailed personal account of their art. (Flipgrid AR is another great tool that can do this easily.) That is AR magic that can have with a meaningful and purposeful impact on students' pride in their own productivity!

XR ABC TOOLBOX

**AR Absorb	HP Reveal**
Updating Textbooks with AR
Tags: social studies, language arts, architecture, science

Platform: iOS and Android devices

Tools: HP Reveal allows teachers or students to create or view AR experiences that blend the physical and digital using a mobile device's camera. These Auras can also be created and shared using HP Reveal Studio.

Five Es (STEM)	Four Cs	ISTE Standards for Students
√ **Engage**	√ **Communication**	☐ Empowered Learner
√ **Explore**	☐ Critical Thinking	☐ Digital Citizen
☐ Explain	√ **Creativity**	√ **Knowledge Constructor**
√ **Elaborate**	☐ Collaboration	√ **Innovative Designer**
☐ Evaluate		☐ Computational Thinker
		√ **Creative Communicator**
		☐ Global Collaborator

ISTE Standards for Educators	SAMR	QR Code for Additional Resources
☐ Learner	☐ Substitution	
√ **Leader**	√ **Augmentation**	
☐ Citizen	☐ Modification	
√ **Collaborator**	☐ Redefinition	
☐ Designer		
√ **Facilitator**		
☐ Analyst		

Ready Learner Go!

Add the HP Reveal app to your phone or tablet. Launch the app and create an account. Create your first Aura by following the on-screen prompts.

Where Do We Go from Here?

Bobby Carlton, director of immersive learning for Ready Learner One and a writer for VRScout, carries MERGE Cubes with him so that he can quickly share the power of AR with clients. According to Bobby,

> Educators especially love the MERGE Cube and how it literally changes the classroom. We put a MERGE Cube on each child's desk with a tablet — once kids started to unlock AR experiences they were completely transformed. The classroom was no longer stagnant. Kids were on their feet, excited to interact with the AR image and comparing their image with their friends'. The classroom comes to life and educators are blown away at how a simple device such as the MERGE Cube changed all that in just minutes.

Can you imagine student experiences like this or the experience you launched with your device at the beginning of this chapter happening through glasses instead of tablets? What about contact lenses? Perhaps it's a bit too *Black Mirror* for our liking, but the logical progression of this technology is wearable devices.

Join the Conversation

1. How do AR Absorb activities inspire your instruction?
2. How can AR Absorb benefit multiple learning styles?
3. Why is AR Absorb a good entry-level option for learners?

Continue the conversation with your PLN (professional learning network) by tweeting your responses using the hashtag #ReadyLearnerOne.

3

AR Blend

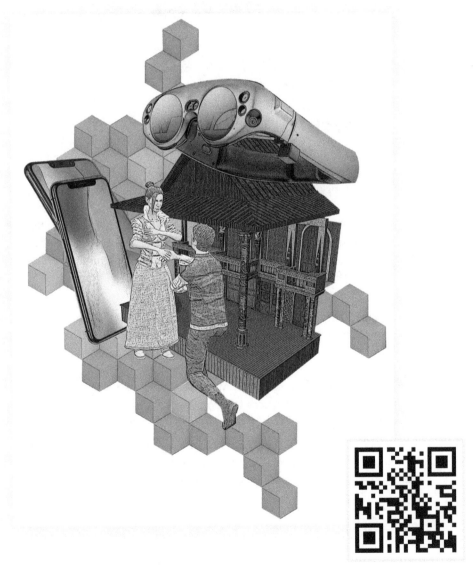

Beyond the Classroom

Coloring books as a new form of meditation? For some people, using coloring books as a method of stress-reduction and mindfulness really works. According to psychologists, coloring increases mindfulness and decreases anxiety. We are seeing a boom in adult coloring books and adult sketchnoting (a form of visual note-taking) for both relaxation and productivity. With three children, my wife and I find coloring provides nice quiet time at home. My kids love to color, and my wife often joins right in. Imagine a peaceful kitchen table with my wife and children coloring away . . . then, enter Daddy, the great disruptor.

I get very excited about how emergent technology like AR can impact our daily lives. So when I found AR coloring books, inevitably quiet time became less quiet. I often print AR coloring pages for my children to color, and when I scan them with a device, my children's work comes to life . . . and so does the kitchen (I have a very patient wife). Custom-colored two-dimensional cartoon characters begin to sing and dance and fly around, and the room fills with delighted laughter as emergent technology puts on a show.

AR coloring books are becoming increasingly popular. My go-to for them is www.quivervision.com, which has apps for a few different categories of AR coloring books, all of which are very engaging.

—Micah

Getting Started

Coloring books are so therapeutic,[1] and now they are animated and interactive. You can color the image to the right like you would in a coloring book (if you are brave enough to write in a book) and see it come to life in AR. There is also a link at the bottom of this section for more free pages to print on your own.

1. Download and open the QuiverVision Masks app.
2. Point your camera at the image to the right.
3. Once the AR graphics pop out, you can flip your camera to face you. The mask is now on your face!
4. Open your mouth, close one eye, and watch how your expression is reflected in the mask.

Print out your own masks and give it a try at www.quivervision.com/apps/masks/.

Quiver Masks
QuiverVision.com/Masks

What is AR Blend?

What exactly do we mean by "Blend"? Blend is an in-between state of consuming content with the ability to manipulate it but not to create something entirely new. For example, you might want to bake cookies: using prepackaged refrigerated unbaked cookies would be the equivalent of "blend" baking. You are not creating from scratch but rather manipulating preexisting dough for a particular outcome — in this case baked cookies. In the Quivervision Masks activity, you start with a preexisting coloring-book image. You can use the mask in black and white or you can color it — just like you can eat prepackaged refrigerated cookie dough straight out of the fridge but we all know how awesome they are when baked first. In AR, the Blend experience allows us the opportunity to manipulate elements to change outcomes while working within preexisting content. It is a step beyond simple consumption (Absorb), because manipulation and change takes place. It is engaging for all learners while remaining intuitive to those who feel ill-equipped or intimidated by the challenges of creation.

An excellent example of a tool that capitalizes on the concept of Blend in AR is 3DBear, an app geared toward the art of storytelling. 3DBear is an AR application that allows users to create scenes using premade objects from an in-app library. Dr. Jen Williams, a well-respected education activist and educator, shared how she engaged with 3DBear in her neighborhood in Florida. On a beautiful May weekend morning, Jen decided to take a walk in her neighborhood to get to know 3DBear and create some immersive stories along the way. She began on her back porch, where she started building a dream team of characters on 3DBear. After looking through a range of models including a clown, a fairy, a robot, and a skeleton, Jen settled on the cute little gnome (perfect for her backyard) and recorded him as he danced on the chair next to her. She was instantly inspired by the possibilities of this tool for engaging students in interactive storytelling to bring their ideas to life, especially with the ability to customize and record! After meeting the gnome and watching him play in different areas of her backyard, Jen decided to create some new AR stories as she took a walk.

Along her journey, Jen paused on a nearby street to use 3DBear to take her neighborhood into the future. As our world needs sustainable solutions that are good for people and planet, Jen decided to add some AR elements to her street to make it more environmentally friendly. In her neighborhood of the future, she was able to add in a bike and bike rack on the street corner, solar panels on a neighbor's house, a rideshare car, and a few electric bikes parked in a driveway. Jen began to think about how this tool could inspire her students as they prepared an informative or persuasive essay. They could use 3DBear-created AR videos to support their ideas — allowing for deeper meaning, creativity, and fun!

Jen's experiences with AR Blend are examples of the powerful impact AR can have on how we experience the world around us.

Pop-Culture Connection

Most people think that partaking in an AR experience involves having to wear some type of gear on your head or using a device with a camera like a tablet or phone. But, in truth, augmented reality can be any computer generated images superimposed over the real world.

When it comes to the AR Blend portion of the XR ABC framework, one of the best examples can be found in Steven Spielberg's 2002 movie *Minority Report*. In the film, Tom Cruise's character investigates a crime using a series of holographic computer screens controlled by simple hand motions. With these gestures, he is able to reorganize information, fast-forward, rewind,

and zoom in and out of the scenes he is reviewing. That manipulation of content is what turns this into an AR Blend experience. He is interacting with the AR content rather than simply consuming it. This scene has not only proven to be one of the most memorable from the film but it's been an inspiration to numerous inventors who have been developing ways to create interactive interfaces similar to the one from the movie. In recent years, attempts have been made using both VR and AR to replicate this type of experience for end users. It could be the closest you'll ever get to being in a Spielberg movie!

CLASSROOM CHRONICLES
MAKING LEARNING MAGICAL
WITH 3DBEAR
TISHA RICHMOND

Finding new and exciting ways to bring the joy of learning into the classroom is my passion. There is nothing better than seeing the sparkle in a student's eyes when learning becomes magical. Recently I discovered a digital tool called 3DBear, and my own eyes sparkled as I marveled at all of the incredible ways that this AR app could bring magic into classroom learning. It's awesome!

Anytime I learn about a new digital tool, I think about how it could be brought into the gamified classroom. Over the past five years, I have layered story and game mechanics into my classes to create a gamified classroom experience for my students. I have witnessed the transformative power of gamification and play as well as the immersive and empowering learning experiences they can create. 3DBear is an augmented-reality application that weaves in beautifully with a gamified classroom environment. Let me share a variety of ways that you can integrate this amazing digital tool with gamification.

Strategy #1: Team promotional videos. Building trust and a sense of family is essential in my team-based gamified classroom. Providing experiences for students to bond and learn about each other's passions and unique abilities is critical. Creating team promotional videos with 3DBear is a fantastic way for teams of students to get to know each other. Have each team create a video introducing themselves to the class. Using the app's 3-D letter models, teams can write their team names. Each team member will select a 3-D avatar that best represents them. These avatars can be used in other projects throughout the year. Students can introduce themselves using the video feature, making recordings where they share something that they are passionate about and a unique skill or personality trait they bring to the team. These videos can be either shared with the teacher through a learning-management system or sent directly to a device's screen.

Strategy #2: Secret messages. I love bringing a little mystery into the classroom to pique students' curiosity. Creating a classroom character within 3DBear is a fantastic way to reveal special quests and challenges.

1. Create a classroom avatar and give it a name.
2. Introduce the character to the class at the beginning of the year or semester, explaining that the character will be hidden in various places throughout the school (or even community) and will reveal special clues or secret missions that students can find.
3. Create a series of short videos of the character in different locations sharing a secret message. You could play these videos for the entire class or hide them using invisible links within Google Docs or Slides, or in QR codes that you display in various places around the classroom.
4. When students interpret the secret message and discover the locations of the avatar, they will find a hidden Easter egg that reveals a clue or secret mission that will give them an advantage in the challenge.

Strategy #3: Scavenger hunts. Building onto the idea of secret messages, 3DBear can be an awesome way to create classroom scavenger hunts using a Google Form.

1. Upload a short 3DBear video for different questions with an avatar in various locations sharing a secret message. At the end of the video,

include a short-answer question that, when answered correctly, will provide a code.

2. Hide a question or clue near the location of the avatar.

3. Students have to locate the 3DBear avatar and interpret the secret message to find the hidden clue. Teams solve the clue or answer the question and type the code into the Google Form.

4. When all codes have been entered correctly, the students have completed the scavenger hunt. You can time students' completion and award points or badges to teams that finish first.

Strategy #4: Side quests. The opportunities for students to demonstrate what they have learned in a creative way are endless in the gamified classroom, and 3DBear supports that on a new level. In my classroom, students have opportunities to accept a "side quest" to demonstrate their understanding of the essential questions in a unit. These side quests are optional, however by completing them, students can earn points that help them level up in a gamified classroom. 3DBear is an awesome option for side quests. Using 3DBear, students can use backgrounds and models to demonstrate their learning, similar to building a diorama—but in augmented reality. In addition, they can bring in models through other applications like Thingiverse, truly making the opportunities for creation limitless. Students can also create videos or photos within 3DBear and then bring those creations into other apps to mash their creations together. So many possibilities!

3DBear is an extraordinary AR application that can add magic to any classroom environment through amplified collaboration, creativity, communication, and critical thinking. I know I have just touched the surface of ways that it can be integrated into the gamified classroom. I can't wait to continue exploring the possibilities with 3DBear and augmented reality!

LEVELING UP IN THE CLASSROOM

Imagine how using 3DBear can allow students the opportunity to build digital storytelling experiences in a plethora of content areas. For example, in a history classroom, students can use 3DBear to re-create a historically significant moment. This can be used for reflection on the impact of that particular moment in history or, by infusing in a language-arts classroom, it can be used as a rewriting-history learning experience: students can alter the outcomes of history and reimagine the moment in a way that has a different societal and cultural impact. Another great way to incorporate 3DBear is in the study of community. Have students design accessibility measures for folks with physical limitations for the various buildings in your community (e.g., library, police station).

XR ABC TOOLBOX

AR Blend | 3DBear

Making Learning Magical with 3DBear

Tags: storytelling

Platform: Requires iOS 9.0 or later. Compatible with iPhone, iPad, and iPod touch.

Tool: 3DBear allows students the opportunity to design scenes using objects from the 3DBear library in augmented reality.

Five Es (STEM)	Four Cs	ISTE Standards for Students
√ **Engage**	√ **Communication**	√ **Empowered Learner**
☐ Explore	√ **Critical Thinking**	☐ Digital Citizen
☐ Explain	☐ Creativity	√ **Knowledge Constructor**
√ **Elaborate**	☐ Collaboration	√ **Innovative Designer**
☐ Evaluate		☐ Computational Thinker
		√ **Creative Communicator**
		☐ Global Collaborator

ISTE Standards for Educators	SAMR	QR Code for Additional Resources
☐ Learner	☐ Substitution	
√ **Leader**	√ **Augmentation**	
☐ Citizen	☐ Modification	
☐ Collaborator	☐ Redefinition	
√ **Designer**		
√ **Facilitator**		
☐ Analyst		

Ready Learner Go!

Download the 3DBear app onto your mobile iOS device and visit the 3DBear website to sign up for a thirty-day free trial of the tool. Imagine you wanted to make your home, or classroom, more accessible for folks with physical limitations. Using the app, create accessibility features for your home.

CLASSROOM CHRONICLES
DYSLEXIA AND CATCHY WORDS AR
JAIME DONALLY

My daughter has dyslexia. She has struggled in particular areas of school, and we've spent countless hours practicing spelling words. We have tried many traditional ways of memorizing spellings, including her writing down a word ten times and then spelling it out loud ten times. We came to a breaking point one night when she was struggling with one word in particular that she couldn't seem to remember.

We tried a new app that had come out called Catchy Words AR that allowed her to play a game similar to hangman but in 360°. Using augmented reality, she was challenged to capture twisted letters in space and put them into a specific order while walking around. Although it took her quite a while to solve the puzzle, when I asked her to spell the word, she was able to do so perfectly. A day later I asked her again, and she was still able to spell the word correctly. A week passed, and she was still able to spell the word.

Why was this method of learning so useful for my daughter? I know that getting up and being active in her learning helped her enjoy the activity and retain the information. I also believe that having to really think about each of the twisted letters and problem solve how to put them in the correct order supported her in memorizing the words. Because her brain was working so hard, the word was stored in long-term memory so that she didn't have to labor that much again.

I'm thankful my daughter found a resource that suits her needs in a way she prefers to learn. With AR and VR we have access to many more personalized activities that can benefit all our students with individualized learning opportunities.

LEVELING UP IN THE CLASSROOM

Remember the days of scavenger hunts? Students would take off around the classroom for clues that connected to the concepts they were learning. Catchy Words is an AR literacy scavenger hunt. Letters float around the students, who must find and catch them with their devices and then arrange the letters into words. Catchy Words can be played with a predetermined set of words or users can add words that connect to a particular area of study. Imagine you are teaching students about the fifty states in a social-studies classroom. With students working in pairs, student A can type "Alabama" into Catchy Words then disperse the letters. Student B can then catch the letters and assemble the name of the state, encouraging recall of the state name and proper spelling conventions. In an elementary classroom focusing on word study, pairs of students can work to enter words that reflect letter blends and then test each other's ability to assemble words following spelling conventions. Catchy Words is an engaging kinesthetic way of increasing competency in spelling.

XR ABC TOOLBOX

AR Blend | Catchy Words AR

Dyslexia and Catchy Words AR

Tags: language arts, spelling, dyslexia, special education

Platform: iOS

Tool: Catchy Words AR is an AR app that engages learners in assembling words from letters.

Five Es (STEM)	Four Cs	ISTE Standards for Students
√ **Engage**	☐ Communication	√ **Empowered Learner**
☐ Explore	√ **Critical Thinking**	☐ Digital Citizen
☐ Explain	☐ Creativity	√ **Knowledge Constructor**
☐ Elaborate	☐ Collaboration	☐ Innovative Designer
√ **Evaluate**		√ **Computational Thinker**
		☐ Creative Communicator
		☐ Global Collaborator

ISTE Standards for Educators	SAMR	QR Code for Additional Resources
☐ Learner	☐ Substitution	
☐ Leader	☐ Augmentation	
☐ Citizen	√ **Modification**	
☐ Collaborator	☐ Redefinition	
☐ Designer		
√ **Facilitator**		
☐ Analyst		

Ready Learner Go!

Download the free Catchy Words AR app.

Engage first with the app using the preset words. Using your device, pop the bubble that contains the letters. Using the device like a magnet, catch the individual letters and place them into the boxes that you see in the lower portion of your screen.

Once you have solved the word, click the plus sign on the top right of the screen and try adding your own word.

CLASSROOM CHRONICLES
CREATING MOMENT
KEVIN CHAJA

I'm pretty much associated with the education field through my wife. She is a school psychologist for the Burbank district, whose school operations were often a topic for our dinner chats. Until 2017, when everything changed.

At the time, I served as executive director of postproduction technologies at Sony in Culver City. I also was tasked with helping with AR/VR for anything from app development to research and development. At a business function, I met the founders of a company called MERGE and saw their new product, the MERGE Cube. I instantly fell in love with this thing. I knew augmented reality was just about to take off, and I saw the MERGE Cube as a different and practical approach. I asked the founders if I could take one home and code some tests on it.

The bulk of my wife's job responsibilities include assessing kids. She has thirty minutes a week for eight weeks to properly assess a child. Almost as soon as she was introduced to the MERGE Cube, she was expressing that she wished the tool could be used to help assess a child. One thing she especially liked was the locked-in immersion and engagement the tool provided, since a child needs to hold the MERGE Cube in front of a device for it to populate the graphics.

I worked with her on defining what she desired the MERGE Cube to be able to provide for her students and began to build a prototype. She needed kids to be able to identify emotions. Since there were six sides to the cube, we narrowed our selection down to sadness, happiness, anger, disgust, fear, and boredom. I was determined. After a day of accessing developer tutorials on Unity—an industry-standard cross-platform game engine that can be used to develop 2-D and 3-D games as well as content for VR and AR—I had a build working with character representations of the six emotions. I showed it to my wife, and she absolutely loved it.

I built the prototype on her phone, and she used it for two assessments the next day. In those two assessments she got key words and comments in much less time than usual from students. The first child, after six minutes, said he didn't want to be "alone" like the sad character on the MERGE Cube. After eight minutes, the next child said she didn't want to be like the fear character, as she was afraid of dying.

This prototype spawned our very first evidence- and research-based app, Moment AR for the MERGE Cube, now patent pending and available on iOS and Android—for free! The app is focused on kids expressing their emotions through the projection of characters onto the MERGE Cube.

By the way, when I first gave my wife the MERGE Cube, she felt it, squished it, and immediately chucked it at the wall. I said, "What in the world are you doing?" She replied, "I just wanted to see if a kid can hurt another kid with it." (It's made of foam, so you can't.) A funny story, but that was the moment when I started paying attention to all the fine details that go into education and special education, and it was the moment I got hooked on designing for educators and kids. That's why I called the app Moment—you get caught in the moment.

You can meet the characters of Moment AR at bit.ly/meetmomentar.

LEVELING UP IN THE CLASSROOM

The Moment AR experience for the MERGE Cube is an excellent resource to support both special education students and general-education students as we promote social and emotional wellness in schools. The Moment AR app allows students who are encountering life challenges and having difficulty verbalizing their emotions to interact with characters they may identify with emotions. This can be parlayed into an opportunity to express emotions through art or writing as an alternative to traditional verbal communications. The tool can be used to support student-counseling sessions and is a great resource for students who don't learn best verbally.

Moment AR also has uses in areas of education outside of special education and SEL (social emotional learning). The app can be used in a foreign-language class to promote conversations in the language of study using an emotional vocabulary. Additionally, the characters in Moment AR can be used in a language-arts class as a writing prompt for storytelling. The possibilities are endless!

XR ABC TOOLBOX

AR Blend | Moment AR

Creation of Moment

Tags: SEL, special education, storytelling

Platform: Requires iOS 9.0 or later. Compatible with iPhone, iPad, and iPod touch. Additionally, the app requires access to the MERGE Cube.

Tools: Moment AR provides learners with an opportunity to explore emotions and feelings. It works with the MERGE Cube.

Five Es (STEM)
- √ **Engage**
- √ **Explore**
- √ **Explain**
- ☐ Elaborate
- ☐ Evaluate

Four Cs
- √ **Communication**
- ☐ Critical Thinking
- ☐ Creativity
- ☐ Collaboration

ISTE Standards for Students
- ☐ Empowered Learner
- ☐ Digital Citizen
- ☐ Knowledge Constructor
- ☐ Innovative Designer
- √ **Computational Thinker**
- ☐ Creative Communicator
- ☐ Global Collaborator

ISTE Standards for Educators
- ☐ Learner
- ☐ Leader
- ☐ Citizen
- ☐ Collaborator
- ☐ Designer
- ☐ Facilitator
- √ **Analyst**

SAMR
- √ **Substitution**
- ☐ Augmentation
- ☐ Modification
- ☐ Redefinition

QR Code for Additional Resources

Ready Learner Go!

Do you have a MERGE Cube? If not, use this image for a glimpse into what is possible.

After loading the Moment AR app on your device, open the app and hold your MERGE Cube in front of your screen. Rotate the cube in your hands to find the emotion character with which you most identify in the moment. Hopefully it will be the happy character, since you must be thrilled to learn about this new example of AR Blend!

Where Do We Go from Here?

The workplace is rapidly changing, and so too are expectations about how our students will use new technologies as part of their day-to-day work flows. Companies like DAQRI are designing new products that leverage the power of AR to increase work efficiency in various workplace settings.[2]

DAQRI has demonstrated a pair of AR glasses that can be worn in the workplace to provide a kind of mutual screensharing. The glasses use a camera to send a worker's point of view to someone at a help desk, and a help-desk person appears in a pop-up window in the worker's glasses. But the functionality doesn't end there: the help-desk person has the ability to make annotations that appear in the worker's glasses—overlaid on the real world through the lenses. It is a really amazing technology that has the potential to positively impact our world.

Imagine the implications of this technology on an aging workforce. Retired experts could support the training of newer employees as consultants who never have to leave home. A new form of apprenticeship training can be implemented.

In our classrooms, AR Blend is an opportunity to help kids get up and out of their seats to explore and engage with the world around them by augmenting learning with content-rich experiences. Plenty of research points to physical activity's positive impact on learning.[3] AR Blend experiences are a perfect fit.

Join the Conversation

1. How do AR Blend experiences inspire your instruction?
2. How do you engage your students with activities that are similar to the AR Blend activities in this chapter?
3. How can you use AR Blend in your classroom?

Continue the conversation with your PLN by tweeting your responses using the hashtag #ReadyLearnerOne.

4

AR Create

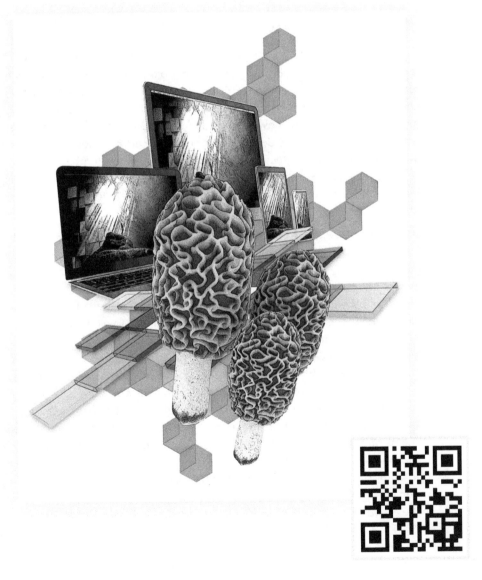

Beyond the Classroom

My daughter loves to make art. At the very earliest stages of her life, she would mix food on her plate and call it art. As she matured a bit, she would begin using crayons and washable paints to create amazing works that she told us were family portraits or beautiful landscapes (some more identifiable than others). Once she was in school, she was in her glory. She'd come home each day with an art project somewhat crumpled in her backpack but—regardless of its state—always headed for the refrigerator door. The most amazing thing about her art was how it evolved as she grew older. Her perspectives changed, her attention to detail became more honed, her choice of subjects became more meaningful, and there was much greater depth in what she was representing. Perspective was the key. Art is all about perspective. It is how we see what we are seeing and how our hearts and minds interpret that visually.

At the XR for Change Festival in New York City in 2019, one of the keynote speakers was artist Nancy Baker Cahill. After spending years and years creating art through traditional modes, she was introduced to creating art in virtual reality. She spoke about how the ability to create art in VR and to examine one's art from a variety of perspectives allowed her to see her art through an entirely new lens. In a quest to allow this same liberty to all people, and not just those who are privileged to have access to the high-end VR equipment on which her art was being created, she developed the idea for the AR app 4th Wall. Through 4th Wall (which is free), users can call up a piece of Nancy Baker Cahill's VR-created art and overlay it on their existing reality (that is, using AR). Viewers can then maneuver through the art to examine it from different perspectives, just as the artist herself can in VR. What impresses me the most about this app is its ability to capture both still images and video footage while exploring the art. I chose to overlay a piece called *Hollow Point 101* in my son's bedroom. I was able to capture images of his name appearing behind, in, and through the art, thereby creating a whole new perspective on the artwork. It was both a privilege and an adventure to access this incredible art through AR and to bring it into my world in a meaningful way.

—*Christine*

Getting Started

Before we jump in, give the 4th Wall AR experience a try. On your device, go to https://www.4thwallapp.org/ or use the QR code below.

If you're thinking about skipping ahead without doing this, don't. You won't want to miss the chance to explore the art created by Nancy Baker Cahill. It's amazing!

Note: This experience requires you to use your device's camera.

What is AR Create?

When talking about learning experiences we want for our students, we often say that we want them to create rather than consume. It can initially be hard to envision that possibility in terms of augmented reality since so much of the content seems premade, which lends itself to either Absorb or Blend experiences. And while we understand the value that those types of experiences provide, we also understand that having students create their own content allows different mind-sets and abilities to be used. But educators sometimes underestimate the power that designing and creating custom experiences for their students can have. When educators design activities for their students with thought and intention, they often elevate the types of thinking that their students are required to do and, in turn, create more impactful learning experiences.

John Dalgety, an educator from Syracuse, NY, found a way to leverage AR technology to create an innovative learning experience for his students at a local event. John had been using Metaverse, an AR creation platform in class, to give students an AR experience that allowed them to learn content in a completely new way. Metaverse allows users to overlay objects, scenery, characters, and animations onto the physical world where people can then interact with them. The local minor-league baseball team, the Syracuse Chiefs, hosts an annual education day for students, and John wanted to use Metaverse and the power of AR to create an engaging experience for his students at the ballpark. He created a game where eight QR codes were placed around the stadium. When students found one of the QR codes and scanned it with their devices, they were presented with an AR experience that assessed them on various school subjects — and baseball. Students who answered all eight questions correctly were entered into a contest to win a prize pack of tickets to return to the stadium another day.

As John put it: "They were looking around the stadium for clues to get the questions. The best part was that they got the full experience without leaving their seats. It was an opportunity to see this venue in a completely different way. The students were fully immersed in the baseball experience and they were learning! Immersing our students in their learning is a game changer to create lifelong learning."

Another idea for implementing an AR Create in your school ties in with 3-D printing. Many schools have purchased 3-D printers as part of their makerspaces or STEM programs. Augmented reality can actually enhance 3-D printing initiatives by allowing students to prototype and see their creations in real-life space prior to printing. This type of prototyping can actually help reduce the overall costs associated with these devices as the amount of filament used should be reduced. And while this is a more practical rather than inspiring example of how AR Create activities can enhance student learning, it's just one of the amazing things that can happen when educators use augmented reality in an AR Create experience.

Pop-Culture Connection

While this book highlights some of the amazing uses of AR and VR technologies in the educational space, there's been one particular show that has been highlighting how these technologies could be used to impact society in the future (and it isn't always pretty). That show, of course, is *Black Mirror*. And while each episode usually has a cautionary lesson for viewers, there is no doubt that the technologies themselves the show depicts allow for users to do some pretty incredible things. In the episode "Playtest," we see several different aspects of augmented reality in use. At first, the episode's protagonist plays a game of whack-a-mole through the use of an implanted AR device. This would fit more with an AR Absorb type of experience. But a more advanced version of the technology, described as "adding layers to existing reality," begins to create people or objects that can be physically interacted with. This type of experience would align with the AR Create layer of the XR ABC framework. While examples from *Black Mirror* tend to be dark, there's no doubt that the show does an impressive job showing us what AR Create experiences could be like for us.

///

CLASSROOM CHRONICLES
DIY POKÉMON GO
MICAH SHIPPEE

As teachers, we are constantly looking to keep our content relevant and meaningful to our students. In my social-studies class, I regularly explore ways to improve motivation and increase interest in my students. Very early in my career, I discovered that the effective and efficient use of emergent technology is the secret to increasing student motivation, creating a more productive learning environment, and better preparing students for the future while achieving the mandated content objectives and goals. So in my classroom, we actively try out new things as a way to engage in modification and redefinition (from the SAMR model).

Location-based AR like Pokémon Go brings meaningful content to a location through geolocation data and offers a unique opportunity to highlight aspects of our schools and communities. Each year I take my students to Liverpool Cemetery, a half mile down the road from my school. Buried in the cemetery are locals who lived through much of the American history I teach. We have veterans from the American Revolution, the Civil War, the Spanish American War, and World War II. There's Erie Canal boat captains, a boy who drowned in the canal, local entrepreneurs, and everyday people who lived through America's rich history. One of my favorites is a young woman named Louisiana who was born just after the Louisiana Purchase. My students and I often discuss the possibility that her parents were excited about westward expansion and Manifest Destiny.

I wanted to transform our annual class cemetery walk by having the students collaboratively research, photograph, and digitally label gravestones in the Liverpool Cemetery. Guided by the work of former local teacher Claire Deloria's *Liverpool Cemetery: A Walking Tour*,[1] students visited the cemetery and photographed and transcribed their assigned gravestone. Next, they completed a collaborative Google Map complete with historical profiles for over thirty gravesites. When a pin is clicked, it reveals a historical profile in images and text detailing what happened in American history when the grave's occupant was alive.

Seeking to take the cemetery-mapping project a step further, we investigated the use of AR programs with Google Map content. We exported the students' custom Google Map as a KML file and uploaded it into Wikitude for use as an AR application. The Wikitude app allows visitors to the cemetery to see where gravesites are located, how far they have to walk to see them, and the historical profiles for each site.

The Liverpool Cemetery project was my first attempt at employing AR technology in our classroom. Once students authored a Google My Map and exported the data to be viewed in AR via smartphones, visitors to the cemetery could download a free app and view the student-created content. Community engagement through innovative learning—a win in the educational space.

LEVELING UP IN THE CLASSROOM

Educators can leverage location-based AR at their schools by thinking about the types of real-world experiences that could benefit from this technology. For example, K–12 teachers have created walking tours of their schools for incoming students and college professors have used them to create tours of their campuses.

There are two different approaches to authoring location-based AR content. The first process helps authors to create a KML file, which is used to create geolocation data. In a DIY collaborative map (for this AR process), authors can collaborate on Google My Maps and then export the content, like in the cemetery example above. The end product is a set of gray pins with text and image content.

The second DIY process for more detailed locations builds off of the collaborative map to include active hyperlinks and images. This can be a bit confusing to try immediately, so I suggest trying the collaborative map first. To build the KML file necessary to complete this process, visit http://geteach. com/arml/. The website was developed by Josh Williams (a brilliant geography educator in Austin, Texas) to deliver a more powerful location-based AR experience.

XR ABC TOOLBOX

AR Create | Google My Maps and Wikitude
DIY Pokémon Go
Tags: social studies, history, field trips

Platform: iOS and Android devices

Tool(s): Google My Maps, Wikitude

Google My Maps, like a Google Doc, allows users to collaborate on one project. This feature can be turned on and off.

Once complete, the map can be exported as a KML file to be imported into Wikitude.

Wikitude's developer website allows users to import KML files (which are geotagged) into their software to view in their free app.

Five Es (STEM)
√ Engage
√ Explore
√ Explain
√ Elaborate
☐ Evaluate

Four Cs
√ Communication
√ Critical Thinking
√ Creativity
√ Collaboration

ISTE Standards for Students
☐ Empowered Learner
☐ Digital Citizen
√ Knowledge Constructor
√ Innovative Designer
☐ Computational Thinker
√ Creative Communicator
☐ Global Collaborator

ISTE Standards for Educators
☐ Learner
☐ Leader
√ Citizen
√ Collaborator
☐ Designer
☐ Facilitator
☐ Analyst

SAMR
☐ Substitution
☐ Augmentation
√ Modification
√ Redefinition

QR Code for Additional Resources

Ready Learner Go!

Create a simple Google My Map of three points near your current location. They should only be a short distance away from you. Export the map as a KML file (by clicking on the three dots) and import it into Wikitude's developer webpage. Once you have completed the Wikitude steps, open the app and see your work by searching for your project title. It should look something like this: bit.ly/GoogleMapARproject.

CLASSROOM CHRONICLES
METAVERSE IN ELEMENTARY MUSIC
CHERIE HERRING

Metaverse, when used in elementary music classrooms, is an exciting learning experience. The free AR platform is being used by thousands of teachers to build all kinds of interactive learning experiences for their classrooms. It is easy to create AR experiences with Metaverse without needing to write any code. That's the best part about using Metaverse with students—it is easy!

There are several ways I've used Metaverse with my students this year, but in this story, I'll focus on how I created interactive adventures in the orchestra unit.

As with any integration of technology, it's best to start with the pedagogy. I mapped out what I wanted my students to review or learn about each instrument before I started making the experiences in Metaverse. Once I mapped everything out, I realized that there was enough information to create several experiences per instrument and throw in some creative twists along the way.

Metaverse Studio is the online site for building interactive experiences, and it works on an iPad as well as other platforms. After the experiences are built, a QR code links to activity you've created. With the Metaverse app, simply scanning the QR code activates the Metaverse experience you have created. No prerequisites—that's refreshing!

Because I wanted to do something creative with the QR codes, I chose to add a logo to the QR codes themselves using an online tool. I then created a game of dice with the QR codes: For the clarinet, for instance, I printed out and attached the QR codes for the different experiences to a Rubik's Cube (much sturdier than a paper die would have been) purchased at the dollar store. In class, each group of children received a die for each instrument they could explore with Metaverse. With a roll of the dice, magic happened.

How do we know if something like Metaverse (or any bit of technology) is a gimmick or if it has real pedagogical value? If all an AR app does is overlay a picture I could have shown my students on my interactive whiteboard, what's the point? AR is worthless if it just delivers static information. But augmented reality gave my students an undeniably better experience than if I had just lectured them on the development of orchestral instruments.

Instead of looking at a picture of a black clarinet, I took my students (via 360° video) deep into a forest in Mozambique to hunt for the mpingo tree, whose wood is the color of chocolate, dense, fine-grained, and resistant to cracking when finger holes are drilled. For my students, who are designing their own instruments, understanding the specialness of the wood used to build a clarinet helps them make more informed choices about the construction of their own projects.

Additionally, AR enabled my students to not just hear but experience instruments being played in different genres, from classical to jazz to marching band. How else can I teleport my students to sit in the brass section of a philharmonic orchestra with a 360° view so they can watch the slide trombone and compare it to the trumpet's valves being played? There are so many exciting and interesting things that can be done to create a genuinely transformative experience.

Most likely, at the elementary level, Metaverse experiences will be teacher-created. At least that's how it has been for me this year. However, as with coding with Scratch and Makey Makey, our students can do much more than we realize. Now that I know how Metaverse works, I can lead my students to create their own adventures, and that will change everything.

After one of my classes, I asked my students to tell me what they thought of the Metaverse experiences. Here's what a few of them said:

* "I liked Metaverse because of all of the cool and funny videos it showed. I also liked the roller coaster!"
* "I liked how we could try to find the pictures and sometimes the pictures would run away from us."
* "I loved the quizzes and activities. It was so much fun and it is awesome."
* "I also like it because instead of just tapping a button and starting it, we had to try and find the questions and videos. It was a challenge."
* "I loved Metaverse because it gives you fun facts about instruments and it is kind of like Pokémon Go."
* "My favorite thing was watching the 360 people play the trombone. I didn't know there were different sizes."

AR experiences are not just a gimmick; they transform the learning opportunities in my elementary music classroom. It takes my students deeper in their understanding and wider in their exposure by bringing everything imaginable into their view.

LEVELING UP IN THE CLASSROOM

In Metaverse, sounds — as well as images, GIFs, videos, and 360° videos — can be added to experiences. Questions can be asked, polls can be taken, and so much more. There are so many features available to build an experience around!

Even better than these features? Teams of students can create their own experiences with instruments (or anything else) and share them with their classmates. Research, mind-mapping, planning, "if-this-then-that," logic — these are just a few of the skills students will use when they build things they can see, use, and play with immediately.

Imagine learning about composers and musicians and having them begin playing right in the middle of the room. One can use augmented reality to tell a story and create background music in GarageBand or use a green screen to add video of children singing or playing the recorder as part of a learning adventure. With the geolocation feature, students can even create a scavenger hunt for hidden instruments or clues around the school. The possibilities are limitless!

QUICK TIP

Do you love art? Would you like to have your own Monet in your classroom? You can leverage Google Arts & Culture to create brand new, location-based perspectives on art by placing them anywhere. With Google Arts & Culture you can virtually visit over 1,200 museums, galleries, and institutions in seventy countries. You can also zoom in on artwork in amazing detail — right down to the brushstrokes! This app also allows you to create your own collections to share with students. After you download the Google Arts & Culture app, click on the camera button. For the AR art experience, select "Art Projector." The app will direct you to scan a flat surface (like the floor), then select a piece of art to view. The art will automatically appear in your space. To foster conversations around place and presence when discussing art, use the small image icon on the screen to add and remove a white background to the art. Imagine viewing incredible garden artwork while in an actual garden! You can start exploring with your students now by bringing the art right into your classroom!

XR ABC TOOLBOX

**AR Create	Metaverse**
Metaverse in Elementary Music
Tags: music, fine arts, creating

Platform: iOS, Android devices, and internet browser

Tools: Metaverse is a mobile and web platform for creating AR experiences. Creating is easy using the storyboard in the Metaverse Studio (studio.gometa.io). Find tutorials on their home page. There are hundreds of scenes and blocks that can be combined to create almost any experience.

Five Es (STEM)	Four Cs	ISTE Standards for Students
√ **Engage**	√ **Communication**	☐ Empowered Learner
☐ Explore	√ **Critical Thinking**	☐ Digital Citizen
☐ Explain	√ **Creativity**	√ **Knowledge Constructor**
☐ Elaborate	☐ Collaboration	√ **Innovative Designer**
☐ Evaluate		√ **Computational Thinker**
		☐ Creative Communicator
		☐ Global Collaborator

ISTE Standards for Educators	SAMR	QR Code for Additional Resources
√ **Learner**	☐ Substitution	
☐ Leader	☐ Augmentation	
☐ Citizen	☐ Modification	
☐ Collaborator	√ **Redefinition**	
√ **Designer**		
☐ Facilitator		
☐ Analyst		

Ready Learner Go!

Download the Metaverse app on a device then scan the code to the left with the app.

CLASSROOM CHRONICLES
MAKING THE WORLD
YOUR STORYTELLING PLAYGROUND
JESSE LUBINSKY

Almost all of my favorite activities to share with educators to help them enhance teaching and learning in the classroom involve what I believe is one of the most powerful art forms: storytelling. There are so many ways to use stories with our students, ranging from having them simply compose their stories on paper to something a bit more elevated like using a slideshow, which not only allows for images to be used but also for the ability to create Choose Your Own Adventure type stories with multiple branching-off points. I love it when teachers challenge their students to research a topic, using a tool like Google Arts & Culture, and then have them create a gallery of artifacts they can use for a formal presentation: rather than create bullet points or narratives for their slides, students simply show their images and tell the story of how the items fit into the topic they were studying. And while there are numerous ways to have students tell stories to demonstrate their learning, there is no doubt that augmented reality has given us the ability to do it in a more powerful way than ever before.

One of my favorite tools for elementary students to create stories is Toontastic 3D. Using this fun app, students can draw, animate, and share cartoons. They can choose from a gallery of objects and move them around against preselected backgrounds, recording audio for their characters and finally saving their story as a video. But one of the things that always struck me about this app was that our students' imaginations were limited to the backgrounds and objects provided by the app. Well, what if there were a way to make the real world a background for your story and to place characters wherever you want? Using the following work flow, you can do just that through the power of augmented reality. (There are many ways to go about creating the images, but I'll go through an iPad-based work flow to demonstrate how this can all be done with just one device.)

You'll need students to be able to access the Keynote and AR Makr apps. First, you will have students create a new Keynote file using a blank template. Each image that you or your students want to add to the AR layer must be placed on a separate slide. You'll want to center each image (which can be things like shapes from the library or pictures that you import) along the bottom of the slide. Be sure to remove any other objects that you don't need, such as extraneous text boxes from the slide deck. Once all your images are set in place, you must make sure to set the background to "no fill" and then export all of the slides as PNG files. Because of the "no fill" background setting, all of the exported images will be transparent, which is exactly what we want for our AR experience.

Now that we have our images, it's time to create the AR experience. Open the AR Makr app and begin to stage your scene by first finding the area where you plan to record and tapping to indicate that you have your location set. You'll then add all of the images you've saved in Keynote to the scene by adding each one individually and placing them at the locations you'd like them to appear in your scene. Once all of your images are placed where the students want them and they are resized to scale, you can hit the record button and create your AR movie!

LEVELING UP IN THE CLASSROOM

It's one thing to be able to create a story digitally with an image for your background, but imagine the power in allowing students the opportunity to create stories in real-life locales that they may be studying in class. Take, for example, a history-related field trip. Students can create their characters and images prior to the trip and have them ready to go. Once on site, you can provide them with time to create their AR stories in the actual places they've been researching. Think about a famous battle site or the location of a historic speech. There are an infinite number of possibilities, and with a little planning, even the most frequently visited spots can become places where student imagination can thrive.

XR ABC TOOLBOX

AR Create | AR Makr
Making the World Your Storytelling Playground
Tags: storytelling, student voice, creating

Platform: iOS

Tool: AR Makr is a creative toolbox for augmented reality. Users can sketch, scan, and snap the world around them and transform their creations from 2-D to 3-D virtual objects. Users can place their creations anywhere in their environment and then record, save, and share their scenes.

Five Es (STEM)	Four Cs	ISTE Standards for Students
√ **Engage**	√ **Communication**	☐ Empowered Learner
☐ Explore	☐ Critical Thinking	☐ Digital Citizen
√ **Explain**	√ **Creativity**	√ **Knowledge Constructor**
☐ Elaborate	☐ Collaboration	√ **Innovative Designer**
☐ Evaluate		☐ Computational Thinker
		√ **Creative Communicator**
		☐ Global Collaborator

ISTE Standards for Educators	SAMR	QR Code for Additional Resources
☐ Learner	☐ Substitution	
☐ Leader	√ **Augmentation**	
☐ Citizen	☐ Modification	
☐ Collaborator	☐ Redefinition	
√ **Designer**		
☐ Facilitator		
☐ Analyst		

Ready Learner Go!

Download the AR Makr app. Try creating a scene with some of the built-in characters. Record a story once you've placed your characters.

Where Do We Go from Here?

There is no question we will see rapid advancement over the next several years in the area of creation through augmented reality. Ben Kelly, a middle school teacher at a rural school in New Brunswick, Canada, had already been using his Microsoft HoloLens to enhance learning in his classroom for some time when he found new uses for it. Ben used HoloTours, which allowed students to visit both Rome and Peru with a tour guide who was so good that the teacher felt like looking for a way to leave a tip. But when Ben discovered one of the first HoloLens mixed-reality apps created by Lifeliqe, he knew right away it marked the death of the textbook industry. Strapping on the tetherless HoloLens allowed Ben's classes to explore STEM, history, and other curriculums in a floating augmented-textbook experience with built-in 3-D models and animations that students could place on tabletops and in nature. Lifeliqe allowed students to capture these AR miracles in video or pictures and use them in their projects. The physics, weather, biology, and chemistry lessons were structured beautifully and supported with over three hundred AR and 3-D models. (*Note: Lifeliqe software is now available on many different devices.*)

Could it get any better? Of course! Using Trimble's SketchUp program, Ben's students designed tiny houses that later would become wooden models and then real $27,000 tiny houses built by his school's skilled-trades students. One piece that was missing was the ability for students to review their 3-D designs in an authentic way and in realistic sizes. SketchUp had a $1,500 HoloLens app that was far beyond his school's budget. Ben reached out to SketchUp to ask if there were any discounts available, and they provided him with the software for free with the condition that all of the incredible learning that was to follow was shared with their company. Ben agreed and began one of the biggest highlights of his career. He and his students were using cutting-edge industrial mixed-reality technology from Microsoft embedded into skilled-trades initiatives that were a first in his part of the world. At that point, Ben and his fellow skilled-trades teacher Michael Robertson looked at each other and knew they had arrived at an educational utopia.

Ben found that every single user had the same reaction when opening their eyes in the HoloLens the first time: their jaws dropped and they said, "wow!" He knew that the Microsoft HoloLens would change learning forever. As Ben put it, "I realize now these are still very much industry devices but when personalized learning becomes our norm and students' interests become our primary curriculum, please know that the devices exist that can transform any learning space into the stuff of legends . . . When the world catches up to this revolutionary technology, everyone will be smiling as wide as I am daily." We expect that AR experiences will continue to allow educators and students to create incredible content to enhance teaching and learning just as it has for Ben and his students.

Join the Conversation

1. What current instructional strategies can you substitute with an AR Create lesson?
2. How can AR Create activities help you redefine your instruction?
3. In what ways can AR Create inspire student productivity?

Continue the conversation with your PLN by tweeting your responses using the hashtag #ReadyLearnerOne.

5

VR Absorb

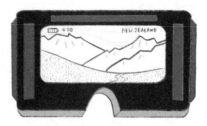

Beyond the Classroom

Last spring, I had the distinct honor of hosting a visiting international school leader from New Zealand who was curious to learn about the educational culture and structure of the US. As we were discussing the lives and experiences of the students in our countries, the vast geographical differences made it challenging to authentically relate to the context of the conversation. That is, until we found a way to make things more relevant. How? At one point, we got to talking about the desire to empower our students to take learning beyond the physical boundaries of the classroom walls. I explained how our district has committed to having students access their learning through VR experiences. I asked the visitor if he would like to give the equipment a go, and he readily complied. As we launched Google Earth, I began to explain how we intend to partner with other schools around the world to participate in collaborative units of study and we hope that our students will become entrenched in global awareness by being able to virtually visit the city/town/village in which the collaborating class resides via the VR equipment. As we discussed this initiative, I asked the visitor if he could, using the VR equipment, take us to his hometown in New Zealand. That's when the magic happened.

After spending close to ten hours together, including four car rides, three meals, and countless conversations, it was by putting on the VR headset and having Chris navigate me through New Zealand for a virtual tour of his homeland that I was able to truly understand who he was and where he came from. It was absolutely magical to virtually walk the roads of his village, fly over his school, and tour the town where he grew up and the farm from which one of his students travels over one hundred miles per day to attend school. It was authentic and customized, and it allowed for me to make a deep personal connection to the international visitor. It helped me understand who he is and what makes him unique. I realized the power that the VR experience brought to my time with him and, in turn, the power that the VR experience will bring to our learners and to our teachers throughout the school year. The ability to create such an emotionally charged, immersive learning opportunity for students that reaches far beyond mere content is powerful and inspiring.

—Christine

Getting Started

Check out this sweet VR Absorb experience to whet your appetite. On your device, go to https://speaktogo.withgoogle.com/ or use the QR code below. You can view the experience with a VR headset such as Google Cardboard or from a laptop.

Note: This experience will use your device's microphone.

What is VR Absorb?

Have you ever wanted to visit a place but the cost and inconvenience of travel was just too much of a burden? The word "tourist" entered the English language after 1800 to describe a member of the mobile community of spectators who sought to explore the world through increasingly accessible museums, repositories of the world's treasures.[1] People flocked to museums to catch a glimpse into the lives of others both past and present. One can hardly condone all the methods used to procure these treasures, but bringing them to the masses truly made previously inaccessible places around the world understandable. Now is the age of the digital tourist, a time when we can explore both real and fictional places as far as other planets from our couches or our classrooms. We can see what others see and walk where others walk. As digital tourists we can begin to empathize, through virtual experiences, and begin a rich and beautiful narrative about the experiences of others.

VR Absorb means visiting distant places and seeing things with your own eyes from the perspective of someone who has been there. VR Absorb experiences are WYSIWYG, meaning the interactivity level is pretty low, with viewers doing just one thing: viewing. We should not dismiss these types of experiences. Simple VR Absorb field trips can be incredibly powerful when paired with meaningful conversations and thoughtful instructional delivery.

Our favorite examples have to do with our children all visiting the same place virtually for the first time. When Micah put his son Tripp (then three years old) on Google Cardboard for the very first time, he asked him to check out the Google Street View 360° imagery in the app. After initiating the experience, Micah asked him, "Tripp, what do you see?" He lifted his head (with the cardboard strapped on) and thought for a few seconds about how to describe what he was seeing. Finally he said: "Daddy, I see an iron mountain." Perplexed, Micah asked him to describe it a bit more, and Tripp repeated that it was an "iron mountain." Confused within the context of his adult understanding, Micah asked for the Google Cardboard so he could see what his son was looking at. When he finally saw Tripp's iron mountain, he realized that it was, in fact, the Eiffel Tower. What a fresh, unfiltered perspective! When Jesse's daughter Jordan, who is an aspiring pastry chef, asked what Paris looked like, he showed her the Eiffel Tower. On her own, she quickly realized that not only could see the monument in all of its glory but she could navigate through the streets as though she was actually there among some of the most famous French bakeries in the surrounding neighborhood. As teachers and parents, it is moments like these that get us excited about exploring the possibilities of emerging technology like virtual reality in the classroom.

Silvia Scurracchio, an educator in Brazil, shared another powerful example of VR in her school. When Silvia was teaching her three- and four-year-olds about life under the sea, her plan was to take her students under the sea with VR. But first they built cardboard submarines! Once the subs were complete, the students entered them and went under the sea with their VR headsets. Silvia's story represents true out-of-the-box instructional practice that takes VR Absorb experiences and profoundly multiplies their impact with meaningful delivery. Building a submarine prior to going into VR is a great example of understanding your students and planning a lesson that focuses on their learning rather than on one tool.

Pop-Culture Connection

Virtual reality has been a major part of the movies for decades. Back in the early 1980s, the cult classic *Tron* featured a main character who becomes digitized and enters into a virtual world. The 1990s featured *Total Recall*, where virtual memories of vacations can be implanted into a person's mind, and *The Lawnmower Man*, an adaptation of a Stephen King story about a gardener with a learning disability who gets supernatural powers after being exposed to a virtual world. But one of our favorite demonstrations of VR Absorb happens in a blink-and-you'll-miss-it moment from the 2001 Pixar film *Monsters, Inc.*, when the monsters are shown using the latest and greatest technology to train to scare children. A monster is connected to a VR headset on the television behind him, and we get a glance of the virtual bedroom he's exploring while being tested on how well he can scare a child. The monsters are simply interacting with the training module, not remixing content within the environment or creating any new content, making this a VR Absorb experience. In fact, many companies, including Walmart, Johnson & Johnson, Farmers Insurance, and Ford, have begun implementing similar VR training experiences for their employees.[2] Minus the monsters of course!

CLASSROOM CHRONICLES

DARWIN AND THE GALAPAGOS ISLANDS
BRIAN CAUTHERS

Let's journey into a typical biology class where the focus is about Charles Darwin and his theory of natural selection for evolution. Charles Darwin sailed around the world making observations in the 1800s exploring . . . blah, blah, blah—you are thirteen years old and could care less what some old guy observed almost two hundred years ago. And where are the Galapagos Islands anyway? They look like a tiny speck in the ocean. Another boring day in science!

Can we shift the mind-set of young students who see history and science as so far removed from their world that it is boring? Absolutely! Students will identify something as boring if it is not relatable for them or it seems too far removed from their own lives. We most certainly cannot take all of our students on a trip to the Galapagos Islands off the coast of South America to explore for themselves just like Charles Darwin did in the 1800s. However, with the power of virtual reality, we can temporarily immerse our students into a realistic high-definition, richly colored vision of almost anywhere on the islands. We can transport our students anywhere in the world. Professional and amateur photographers share their 360° images and videos on many platforms so that we can all experience places in the world that previously could only be visited in our dreams.

In my science classroom, my students do not look at black-and-white photocopies of the finches and tortoises that Darwin studied in order to learn about evolution and natural selection. Instead, they use VR apps that allow them to explore images and videos from various locations on the islands and around the world so that they can re-create Darwin's voyage. The students explore, make observations, and compare their experiences in order to draw their own conclusions about the similarities and differences between the vastly different islands and the creatures that inhabit them. For a short period of time, the students actually feel like they can reach out and touch a 150-year-old tortoise. They see the rich landscape, varied terrain, and plant life firsthand. Students venture into the virtual environment alongside the marine iguanas diving underwater to eat algae off of the rocks—a phenomenon that does not happen anywhere else in the world. And they do not have to sail around the world to do it.

They also do not have to beg their parents to spend thousands of dollars to travel. Many of our students do not have the resources or the family structure that can provide them with these once-in-a-lifetime experiences. With the power of virtual reality and photographers from around the world sharing their work, our students can now experience what they never thought was possible. In some cases, it might even inspire them to take on a different career path than previously expected. At the very least, my students do not sit in my class and look at black-and-white handouts thinking, "Who cares about some guy that sailed around the world two hundred years ago?" They explore, ask questions, wonder, scream out in awe as a sea lion swam right next to them, and imagine what it was like to step foot on a remote island with unique features.

LEVELING UP IN THE CLASSROOM

Interested in leveraging virtual reality as a means of taking students on learning adventures that explore the different ecosystems on our planet? Brian's story shows just one of many ways that we can utilize virtual exploration to provide students with an immersive learning experience that allows them to deeply connect with their learning.

Take, for example, theBlu, which is an underwater-diving experience available in virtual reality. After studying the impact that pollution has on the coral reefs of the world, you can have students "dive" into their learning by immersing them in theBlu and having them make observations about the ecosystem around them. Students can then theorize how ocean contamination like oil spills can impact this ecosystem and the results it has on the marine life.

You can also use Google Earth when studying the impact of scarcity of water. By virtually visiting places in Pakistan and India that are densely populated and quickly running out of water supply, students are able to take a concept that is far removed from their own lives and personalize their learning by actually walking in the shoes of those affected by it. Walking through a village in Pakistan or a city in India while exploring the people and culture around them allows students to hypothesize the impact that forced relocation resulting from a lack of water supply will have. There are countless ways that virtual reality can be leveraged to immerse students in a more impactful learning experience.

XR ABC TOOLBOX

VR Absorb	theBlu
Darwin and the Galapagos Islands
Tags: science, environmental

Platform: Oculus Rift, HTC Vive, and Windows Mixed Reality

Tool: theBlu is an immersive VR experience that explores the ocean and its ecosystems.

Five Es (STEM)	Four Cs	ISTE Standards for Students
√ **Engage**	☐ Communication	☐ Empowered Learner
√ **Explore**	√ **Critical Thinking**	☐ Digital Citizen
☐ Explain	☐ Creativity	√ **Knowledge Constructor**
☐ Elaborate	☐ Collaboration	☐ Innovative Designer
☐ Evaluate		☐ Computational Thinker
		☐ Creative Communicator
		☐ Global Collaborator

ISTE Standards for Educators	SAMR	QR Code for Additional Resources
☐ Learner	☐ Substitution	
☐ Leader	☐ Augmentation	
☐ Citizen	√ **Modification**	
☐ Collaborator	☐ Redefinition	
☐ Designer		
√ **Facilitator**		
☐ Analyst		

CLASSROOM CHRONICLES
WALK LIKE AN EGYPTIAN IN VR
STEVE BAMBURY

Not every school has the budget to invest in a large amount of VR equipment. This does not mean that VR experiences cannot be delivered to enrich the curriculum and provide meaningful learning opportunities. As with all types of education tech, as long as you focus on the learning and the skills inherent in the activity, even a limited number of VR headsets can be harnessed effectively.

The example I want to share comes from a project I helped to coordinate for year-3 students at Jumeirah English Speaking School (JESS)—one of the three schools that make up JESS Dubai, where I work as head of digital learning and innovation. The topic that the students were learning about was ancient Egypt (a personal favorite of mine), and I was asked to help the staff integrate some immersive learning experiences into this area of study. This primary school had access to a small bank of seven mobile VR headsets that utilized iPod touches. With a class size of twenty-two, it was clear that not everyone could use a headset at the same time, and the last thing you want is to have students waiting for a turn on something—it would amount to wasted learning time. The math seemed to suggest that I could get a third of the class on the headsets at a time, so logically three activities, coordinated in rounds, would be an ideal way to organize the proceedings. The other two activities needed to be both engaging (i.e., not just boring worksheets while students waited for their go with the VR) and something that students could navigate independently.

I often advise educators new to VR to start small and look to certain key apps like Google Expeditions, Nearpod, and even just YouTube. What all three of these have in common, besides being free, is that they offer great equity in terms of how 360° experiences can be harnessed. All three will work on mobile VR headsets but can also be accessed via tablets, which utilize a gyroscope to let users look around by moving the device. As such, having decided on using the Ancient Egypt VR app by Inspyro with the VR headsets, I chose Nearpod and YouTube as the platforms for the supplemental experiences. I actually wrote some of the original virtual field trips for Nearpod, including one inside the tomb of Rameses VI, so I knew that by launching "self-paced" mode, the students could move through the interactive presentation on their iPads with very little support.

For YouTube I did something that I have done for several departments at JESS Dubai and curated a set of relevant 360° videos in advance then turned the links into a sheet of QR codes for the students to scan. It's crucial that you always vet the content on YouTube before delivering it to students—both to ensure that the content is appropriate and that it is well matched to the students' abilities.

I produced a page with four areas marked out—one for each of the three experiences and a fourth for a photo of the child using the VR to be placed on. For each activity, a follow-on task was set for them on the sheet:

1. Ancient Egypt VR (headsets): Write a description of the tomb that they virtually navigated.
2. Nearpod (iPad): Write their name in hieroglyphics, following from the content in the interactive presentation.
3. YouTube 360 (iPad): Collate a minimum of three facts based on the videos.

Now I had activities that all used immersive technology to varying degrees and tasks that could be completed independently. The final touch was a little extra incentive. At the start of each session (I delivered this four times to four different classes) I showed a clip of the Discovr Egypt VR app. This is a higher-end VR application that actually allows you to walk around inside a re-creation of King Tut's tomb. I explained that we only had one headset that this could run on (my Acer WMR headset) so not everyone would get to try it. But, I said, I and the class teacher would each select one person to come back for a bonus VR session with me the following week and have a go. The way that they could earn a place in this special group was to be the students who put the very best effort into completing the three tasks we were about to set for them. Suffice to say the effort levels went through the roof.

LEVELING UP IN THE CLASSROOM

There are so many incredible opportunities to use VR Absorb in the classroom as a means of exposing students to areas beyond the walls of the classroom. For example, when studying the architecture of ancient amphitheaters, using Google Earth in VR allows students to explore and make observations of the ancient ruins of Greece and Rome. Take the learning to the next level by inviting students to use the same platform to explore the inside of Radio City Music Hall in New York City, and have them compare and contrast the design features to its ancient predecessors. Looking to relate VR Absorb to a language arts class? When having students hone their skills in writing realistic fiction, take them on an adventure through an unfamiliar city and challenge them to use descriptive language in explaining their surroundings. Allow peers to provide feedback on the quality of the descriptive language being used and then have students apply the experience to their writing. Yet another means of embracing VR Absorb is to have students explore artifacts and evidence of history through Inspyro apps, such as Maya ActiveLens, Cold War Nuclear Strike VR, and more. A simple search for Inspyro VR apps will provide you with numerous learning opportunities for students.

XR ABC TOOLBOX

VR Absorb | Ancient Egypt VR

Walk Like an Egyptian in VR

Tags: history, global awareness

Platform: iOS 6.0 or later. Compatible with iPhone, iPad, and iPod touch.

Tool: Ancient Egypt VR by Inspyro allows learners to explore temples in ancient Egypt.

Five Es (STEM)	Four Cs	ISTE Standards for Students
√ **Engage**	☐ Communication	☐ Empowered Learner
√ **Explore**	√ **Critical Thinking**	☐ Digital Citizen
☐ Explain	☐ Creativity	√ **Knowledge Constructor**
☐ Elaborate	☐ Collaboration	☐ Innovative Designer
☐ Evaluate		☐ Computational Thinker
		☐ Creative Communicator
		☐ Global Collaborator

ISTE Standards for Educators	SAMR	QR Code for Additional Resources
☐ Learner	☐ Substitution	
☐ Leader	☐ Augmentation	
☐ Citizen	√ **Modification**	
☐ Collaborator	☐ Redefinition	
√ **Designer**		
☐ Facilitator		
☐ Analyst		

Ready Learner Go!

Interested in learning what other experiences Inspyro has to offer educators and their learners? Do a simple web search for Inspyro VR apps (they also offer a host of AR apps) and choose the one that best fits your learning environment. Begin to think about how this app can engage your learners.

CLASSROOM CHRONICLES
BECOMING HOMELESS, AN EMPATHY-BUILDING VR EXPERIENCE
STEVEN SATO

Virtual reality is sometimes classified as an empathy machine. While I do not disagree that it can drive empathy, or even open our eyes to our own prejudices and judgmental natures, empathy is just one of many powerful attributes of VR. That said, Stanford's Virtual Human Interaction Lab has created an experience entitled Becoming Homeless: A Human Experience to, according to its website, dispel the "misconception that losing one's home is due to who you are and the choices you make."[3] The aim of the experience is to examine how we might blame others for bad things that happen to them but never really consider the reasons things happen to us.

At my school, I have the honor of running our VR elective, and as much as an elective should be fun, this one is also very educational. That was the case when my students got to experience Becoming Homeless.

The experience begins with the user listening to the radio in the app. The economy is going downhill. You lose your job, you sell your assets, you are evicted. You live in your car and are confronted by the police. While on a bus, you try to hold on to your personal belongings while being harassed by a stranger. Finally, everything culminates with the opportunity to listen to real stories from people who have become homeless. You can click on bus passengers and hear their stories about the circumstance that led them to homelessness.

During the elective a student asked me why he was arrested by the police in the app; I asked him to hold on to that question to discuss after the experience. At the end of the experience we had a class discussion about homelessness. I prompted the student to ask the question again, and we collaboratively determined that perhaps someone in the app had called the police on the user.

We asked if anyone had had any encounters with a person experiencing homelessness, and everyone said no. If they noticed a homeless person in a car for an extended period of time on their street would they call the police? Some said yes, some said no. We asked those who answered yes to tell us why. They responded with answers that ranged from "they might be dangerous" to "they must be drug users." Some countered those answers by saying that they were "just stereotypes" and "you don't know their circum-stances"—taking into consideration what they had heard from the people on the bus in the experience.

If we're taking the advice of Jeremy Bailenson, the director of the Virtual Human Interaction Lab, and using VR for the "impossible, rare, expensive, counterproductive, and dangerous," then perhaps this experience falls into the counterproductive. To place students in an environment to do all of the things they did in VR would be a logistical nightmare, not to mention time intensive, costly, and simply impractical. However, through the power of vir-tual reality we were able to condense a powerful set of experiences in an immersive format where strong memories and impact were made. This resulted in a deep, thoughtful discussion and reflections on homelessness and how each of the students perceive it.

I highly recommend this experience and find tremendous value in what Jeremy Bailenson and Stanford's Virtual Human Interaction Lab is doing. It is clear there is incredible value for students in these types of experiences.

LEVELING UP IN THE CLASSROOM

Becoming Homeless: A Human Experience is a powerful opportunity for edu-cators to help students see the world that exists beyond the confines of their own communities. The opportunity for raising global awareness through this experience is monumental. While the experience undoubtedly builds empa-thy for people's circumstances and establishes social awareness, it also goes far beyond that. The Becoming Homeless experience helps dispels prejudices when it comes to the causes or circumstances aligned with a person's social status. This is an excellent resource to use as a means of exploring social reform with students. It can also be aligned to the study of politics and polit-ical sciences. It can be used as a launching pad for a mathematics class to do statistics studies comparing homeless rates in urban areas vs. rural areas or between different global cities; it can also be used to study diversity among homeless populations. It can be used in a science class to determine how climate impacts homelessness. It can be used in a language-arts classroom as a writing prompt or a public speaking assignment for a student to act as an advocate for a character from the experience. Any time that we can take students out of their current surroundings and expose to them to the vaster global community, it is a step toward establishing them as global citizens.

XR ABC TOOLBOX

VR Absorb | Becoming Homeless

Becoming Homeless, an Empathy-Building VR Experience

Tags: social awareness, community engagement, sociology

Platform: HTC VIVE or Valve Index; Windows 8 or higher

Tool: Becoming Homeless: A Human Experience. In this immersive VR experience from Stanford University's Virtual Human Interaction Lab, you can spend days in the life of someone who can no longer afford a home. Interact with your environment to attempt to save your home and to protect yourself and your belongings as you walk in another's shoes.

Five Es (STEM)	Four Cs	ISTE Standards for Students
√ **Engage**	☐ Communication	√ **Empowered Learner**
√ **Explore**	√ **Critical Thinking**	☐ Digital Citizen
☐ Explain	☐ Creativity	√ **Knowledge Constructor**
☐ Elaborate	☐ Collaboration	☐ Innovative Designer
√ **Evaluate**		☐ Computational Thinker
		☐ Creative Communicator
		☐ Global Collaborator

ISTE Standards for Educators	SAMR	QR Code for Additional Resources
☐ Learner	☐ Substitution	
☐ Leader	√ **Augmentation**	
☐ Citizen	☐ Modification	
☐ Collaborator	☐ Redefinition	
☐ Designer		
√ **Facilitator**		
☐ Analyst		

Ready Learner Go!

Close your eyes and imagine what it feels like to have a police car pull out behind you on the highway. Think of that feeling of dread that you inevitably encounter. Now imagine being a homeless teenager who is trying to survive day to day and having that same encounter with the police as you navigate the Becoming Homeless experience.

Where Do We Go from Here?

One VR educational experience, Anne Frank House VR, developed by Oculus and Force Field, gives us some insight into what VR Absorb experiences could look like for students in the near future. Users can tour every room of the secret annex in Amsterdam where Anne Frank and seven other Jewish people hid from Nazis from 1942 to 1944. Every room in Anne Frank's home has been re-created virtually in painstaking detail to provide users with a truly authentic experience. And while it would be easy enough to re-create the home as it is today, various artifacts such as notes and pictures are scattered about the environment to allow users to get a better sense for what it was actually like there at the time Anne Frank lived there.

This type of experience takes the idea of the virtual field trip to a level not possible without VR technology. Virtual field trips have the incredible ability to capture student interest and imagination simply with 2-D images, but imagine allowing your students to go on a virtual exploration of a place with historical context added as well. Any place in any time period can be an option for students to explore and interact with. If Anne Frank House VR is any indication, this is just the very beginning of making these types of experiences readily available. And that could make for some incredible learning experiences that educators can design for their students.

Join the Conversation

1. How do VR Absorb activities inspire your instruction?
2. How can VR Absorb benefit multiple learning styles?
3. Why is VR Absorb a good entry-level option for learners?

Continue the conversation with your PLN by tweeting your responses using the hashtag #ReadyLearnerOne.

6

VR Blend

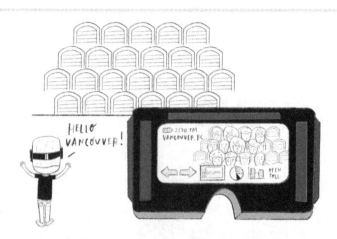

Beyond the Classroom

I consider myself to be a pretty good public speaker. I've done presentations and keynotes around the globe and have gotten to the point where before taking the stage I feel excited rather than nervous. However, I've always had one area that I wish I could improve upon. I am terrible at rehearsing. I mean, I'm always well prepared when it comes to my slides and knowing what I want to say, but I can't just stand in a room and practice to a wall. It's like I have some type of mental block preventing me from doing it. I mentioned this issue to a colleague, and they told me they had been practicing their speeches to virtual audiences. I immediately wanted to try it out when I found that the VirtualSpeech app was available on the Oculus Go I owned.

What I found really helped me up my public-speaking game. Not only could I select from a variety of different settings such as a conference room, presentation space, or large theater but the crowd made subtle movements (as they would in real life) and there were ambient noises that added to the realism. And while the virtual crowd didn't react to any of my jokes (of which there were many), I was able to track how long it took me to get through my talk using my own slides. For those people who really need help with public speaking, the app can also track things such as eye contact with the audience and the use of hesitation words. There are even add-ons such as full courses to help with broader skill sets related to topics like interviewing techniques and delivering sales pitches.

Now, I love this as a tool to refine my own practice, and it's a practical example I love to share of the benefits of virtual reality. It could just be the confidence boost that superstar hiding in plain sight needs to break out of their shell and deliver the next great TED Talk.

—Jesse

Getting Started

Hop right into VR and experience what it is like to have a conversation with people from all over the world in virtual space. There are a few options to experience this:

- **Minecraft:** When entering Minecraft through a mobile app, desktop edition, or game system you can find a multiplayer experience. Sometimes creating your own world and inviting specific people works best. Need some help? Check out the article at http://bit.ly/lifewireminecraft.
- **AltspaceVR:** On a VR headset or Windows PC you can use AltspaceVR (https://altvr.com/). In Altspace you can find categories of events that might pique your interest. (Altspace VR is a social VR platform for users to meet people around the world, attend free live events, and play interactive games with friends.)

What is VR Blend?

Similar to AR Blend, VR Blend is the state of consuming content while manipulating it but not creating something entirely new — but within virtual reality. In VR, Blend allows us the opportunity to manipulate the experience in which we are immersed to change the outcome while working within preexisting content. It is a step beyond simple consumption, or Absorb, because there is manipulation and change taking place in the experience. It is engaging for the learner while intuitive to those who may feel ill equipped or intimidated by the challenges of Create.

VR Blend allows users the opportunity to manipulate experiences to provide for a more meaningful and personalized encounter. Let's use an actual classroom experience to provide context to our understanding. In Water Bears VR, the user is tasked with freeing trapped bears from water bubbles. To do so, the user must use a limited number of tools (pipelines, connectors, etc.) to direct a water flow from its initial point to the bubble in which the bear is trapped. By navigating around the environment in VR, the user is able to examine the situation from various angles and begin the creative problem-solving thought process. Users are challenged to build and rebuild the pipelines to allow the water flow to reach the bears. Testing the user's spatial reasoning, this engaging experience allows for a true use of Blend, since the user is manipulating the environment to solve a puzzle without having to actually create content from scratch. We will see a more intimate exploration of Water Bears VR through the experiences of an educator shared in a story in this chapter.

There are many opportunities available in VR that allow for students to access the skill sets and learning outcomes provided through a Blend experience.

Pop-Culture Connection

While not necessarily the first movie that comes up in discussions of virtual reality, the 1994 film *Disclosure* gives us a rich example of early perceptions of the possibilities of virtual reality. In the film, Michael Douglas's character dons a set of VR goggles and a data glove and enters something called the Corridor, a 3-D visualization of his company's data repository, in order to investigate company records. While in the Corridor, he is able to open, view, and manipulate files much as he would in a desktop environment (which shows that back in the early 1990s, while cool environments could be imagined, people still had trouble envisioning possibilities for VR beyond replacing existing functionalities). Employing VR in this manner — to modify existing content beyond just simple, reactive interactivity with the environment — is a great example of the VR Blend aspect of the XR ABC framework.

CLASSROOM CHRONICLES
BLENDING REALITIES WITH RUMII
AMANDA FOX

There has been a lot of discussion around virtual reality, and with new tech comes myths and even fear of adoption that usually arise from a limited understanding of the technology's breadth and applications. The myth I plan on busting is that virtual reality is an isolating experience. The myth is that once the headset goes on, the real world disappears and the digital reality becomes a solitary one. While that can be true in some circumstances, there are apps and programs that are designed for the completely opposite outcome: social VR. And it can be one of the most powerful experiences that you can bring to your students—one that can allow you to bring your students on educational adventures of epic proportions.

In the last few years, I have explored multiple facets and applications of immersive technologies for student creation in after-school and K–8 settings. I have even been fortunate enough to present on the topic around the world, most recently at the DigiSTEM Conference in Sydney, Australia. And using virtual reality, I was able to remove the veil of the headset and give my audience a peek at what using VR to foster collaboration, creativity, and communication, while defying geography looks like.

Rumii by Doghead Simulations, a VR collaborative-presentation software, enabled me to take three of my sixth-grade immersive technologies students with me to Australia. Well . . . at least their avatars!

After I presented on blending realities while modeling blending virtual and actual reality, my students virtually joined in behind me on the screen to participate in a Q&A panel—as did Amber Osborne, marketing director of Doghead Simulations, and Steven Sato, the director of technology for a K–8 school in Los Angeles. As we talked about VR in education, I modeled the power of presence and empowered my sixth-grade students as VR experts, prompting them to talk about their experiences and the projects they created in VR. How many sixth graders in the USA can say they co-keynoted a conference? Let alone one in Australia!

Prior to leaving for my trip, we experimented with Rumii in our classroom: familiarizing ourselves with the features, functions, and constraints of the platform. Rumii is device agnostic and runs on computers, headsets, and mobile devices like tablets and phones. When I got to Sydney, each of my students joined me in VR the day before for a practice run. Finally, the day arrived for my three rock-star students back in Dallas, Texas, to all jump into Oculus Gos from their respective homes and meet in the virtual conference room to present. I was able to project our meeting room for the audience, and everyone could see my students in avatar form as they ran around in VR creating collaborative drawings on the whiteboard and importing and manipulating 3-D models.

Demonstrating new technologies obviously comes with the risk of it not always working. And sure enough, we ran into sound issues at no fault of the platform. I persevered through the sound issues, trying to problem solve with wires, plugs, and settings to no avail. But even with the sound issues, I heard from several teachers that the students attending the keynote thought that seeing and interacting with students from America was the coolest part of the presentation.

So one word of advice: don't avoid risks because it might cost failure. If everything works, you are bringing an incredible experience to stakeholders participating. More importantly, if it doesn't, you model risk, failure, grit, and how to keep calm during problem solving. In the end, you might have planted the potential for a million use cases and changed the narrative of the hesitant adopter from "I don't know where to start with VR" to "I can start here."

And that is the message I want you to take to heart as you choose to embark on your own VR adventure: choosing a reality in which you are bold and bring experiences like this to students is better than choosing a reality of geographic isolation, of isolating learning to your classroom or your building. Social VR has arrived and it will unabashedly change our current constraints of teaching and learning.

LEVELING UP IN THE CLASSROOM

Use Rumii to help students create engaging presentations and overcome presenter anxiety.

Brian Costello, a middle school teacher, has been teaching students how to present for years. One year Brian decided to let his students choose whether or not to use Rumii for virtual presentations. About half of one of Brian's classes chose to present in Rumii, and the results were fantastic. Students spoke confidently, could be heard easily, and had less anxiety. Their topics? Students shared their visions of technology ten years in the future. They spoke about the future of everything from video games to transportation to schools all while experiencing the kind of platform that will enhance their ability to work with others anywhere in the world in their own futures.

XR ABC TOOLBOX

VR Blend | Rumii

Blending Realities with Rumii

Tags: presenting, speaking

Platform: Oculus Go, Oculus Rift S, Oculus Quest, HTC Vive, HTC Vive Pro, Windows Mixed Reality Headsets, PC, Mac, Steam, and Android

Tool: Rumii is a social VR space that enables people to collaborate and communicate in one virtual room. Users can engage from anywhere in the world as though they are all in the same physical location.

Five Es (STEM)
- √ **Engage**
- √ **Explore**
- ☐ Explain
- ☐ Elaborate
- ☐ Evaluate

Four Cs
- √ **Communication**
- ☐ Critical Thinking
- ☐ Creativity
- ☐ Collaboration

ISTE Standards for Students
- ☐ Empowered Learner
- ☐ Digital Citizen
- ☐ Knowledge Constructor
- ☐ Innovative Designer
- ☐ Computational Thinker
- √ **Creative Communicator**
- √ **Global Collaborator**

ISTE Standards for Educators
- √ **Learner**
- √ **Leader**
- ☐ Citizen
- ☐ Collaborator
- ☐ Designer
- ☐ Facilitator
- ☐ Analyst

SAMR
- ☐ Substitution
- ☐ Augmentation
- ☐ Modification
- √ **Redefinition**

QR Code for Additional Resources

Ready Learner Go!

Visit the Rumii page at https://www.dogheadsimulations.com/.

Download the software to the appropriate device and create a free account, which will allow for a limited number of users. You can always upgrade for more users. Be sure to try it out before rolling it out full scale.

VIRTUAL LABS WITH LABSTER
SUZANNA KATZ

When Staten Island Academy (SIA) became the first high school to use Labster VR last year in a pilot program, I had just started my job at the school, having recently finished my PhD. I was very interested in the intersection between technology and biology, and I really wanted to integrate that into my new experience as a teacher. Labster allowed me to use laboratory simulations to get my advanced-placement biology students excited about the application of complex textbook concepts in a high-tech modern research laboratory.

When I first started as a teacher at SIA, I was told that my longest classes would be relatively short, which naturally made it more difficult to teach AP biology topics. It's a long curriculum that I think is very difficult for most teachers to get through while providing in-depth examples. Our longest class is an hour, and it's very difficult to do certain labs in that time, especially when you don't have the kind of equipment that you see in a university setting. I was determined to expose my students to a high-quality experience, so I began searching for simulations online. I had already heard about virtual reality, so I tried to look for a VR experience that had lab integration.

One of the criteria that was important in my search was how the technology affected my students. I wanted to use a more advanced device because I knew there was a risk of a low frame rate making the students nauseous. It would be a disaster if I gave the kids a device that made them feel sick! I started leaning toward the stand-alone devices from Google because I wanted something that was easy to figure out, didn't have too many moving parts, and could be used without difficulty with my group of kids. I also wanted something that had potential for large-scale adoption, and I felt confident that Google would continue to release content for their devices. That's how I narrowed my search down to the Lenovo Mirage Solo with Google Daydream.

When I saw the Labster app, I thought it would be perfect for our class. So I got in touch with Labster, and our pilot program was born. Things moved very quickly from there. I presented the pilot to our school directors, and they loved the idea of enriching the class experience in this way. The approval process went quickly. I was amazed at how little red tape there was in implementing such a new technology. The next step from there was to find out how the app could be integrated into and aligned with my curriculum. With help from the Labster support team, I realized that I could now get a complicated lab done within one single period or have students able to finish the work at home.

So SIA started the pilot program, making us the first high school to try Labster VR. It was exciting! The kids were particularly excited about it. They'd never seen anything like Labster, and I think they felt really special that they were chosen to try it.

Leveraging different educational technologies, I designed my course with an assortment of tools. My classroom is definitely a mixed-media learning environment. I often start class with a visual or video to introduce students to the topic so they get a feel for the overarching ideas and principles. Then I begin a lecture where I go over the concepts in detail. As we progress in the topic, we'll do in-class exercises or homework to solidify students' knowledge. Once I sense they understand the concepts relatively well we do a simulation. The simulations give students a cohesive view of the topic and expose them to applications of the concepts that would typically only be found in university settings.

I've used the simulations to cover several topics, including evolution, polymerase chain reactions, RNA extraction, viral gene therapy, gene expression, and gene regulation. We've gone through a few simulations, and I found that they really fit with our curriculum. It's been particularly useful for our biotechnologies section, particularly the stem cell culture lab and the viral gene therapy lab, where we covered a range of devices and tools that are not typically available in high-school settings. I definitely can't give students a pluripotent stem cell experience or a viral gene therapy experience in a high-school lab due to the cost and regulations involved in using those technologies. So it's been really helpful for me as a teacher to use the virtual labs to get through topics that require visualization and physical practice. My students are essentially getting a level of experience that I was not exposed to until my thesis work in graduate school.

LEVELING UP IN THE CLASSROOM

By using virtual labs, students are afforded opportunities for immersive hands-on learning in an environment that would be otherwise impossible to provide. One of the most incredible aspects of virtual labs is not just the exposure to learning tasks but also to the tools involved. Think about how we can pair this learning with a language-arts-based writing task or an economical study in math on the cost of operating the same experience in a traditional lab. This learning can be extended to other areas by assessing how beliefs and practices of different cultures around the world can sometimes act as barriers to these types of learning experiences in their conventional forms. By accessing virtual labs, we are yet again eliminating the borders and boundaries of student learning.

XR ABC TOOLBOX

VR Blend	Labster
Virtual Labs with Labster
Tags: science, labs

Platform: Daydream headsets, including Daydream View and the Lenovo Mirage Solo

Tool: Labster is a platform that offers VR biology lab experiences covering the subjects of cell and molecular biology, ecology, and physiology

Five Es (STEM)	Four Cs	ISTE Standards for Students
√ **Engage**	☐ Communication	√ **Empowered Learner**
√ **Explore**	√ **Critical Thinking**	☐ Digital Citizen
☐ Explain	☐ Creativity	√ **Knowledge Constructor**
☐ Elaborate	☐ Collaboration	☐ Innovative Designer
√ **Evaluate**		√ **Computational Thinker**
		√ **Creative Communicator**
		☐ Global Collaborator

ISTE Standards for Educators	SAMR	QR Code for Additional Resources
☐ Learner	☐ Substitution	
☐ Leader	☐ Augmentation	
☐ Citizen	☐ Modification	
☐ Collaborator	√ **Redefinition**	
☐ Designer		
√ **Facilitator**		
☐ Analyst		

Ready Learner Go!

Visit the Labster simulations page at https://www.labster.com/simulations/ and take a look at all of the engaging labs that are offered. Think about how your own experience would have been different if you had had an opportunity to engage in your science studies using this instructional tool when you were in high school. How are today's students benefiting from these emergent instructional technologies?

CLASSROOM CHRONICLES

ON VIRTUAL PINS AND NEEDLES

SAM JANG

As CEO of a VR-platform company, Artificial Intelligence Inc., I recognize the importance of providing a broader view of what learning experiences in VR will be like for our K–12 students as they enter higher education. Even acupuncture, which has been a hallmark of traditional Chinese medicine for over two thousand years, can now benefit from the unique learning environments made possible by VR. Acupuncture has rather recently gained widespread acceptance for its efficacy in treating a patient's pain symptoms and health imbalances, though it was once considered pseudoscience by providers of Western medicine. It seems the energy meridians and the acupoints that enable their manipulation were considered mysterious because they couldn't be observed through traditional scientific methods. With the aid of VR, students can now grasp the complexity of the human body in a visually stimulating immersive environment. If seeing is believing, VR has the power to make believers out of medical skeptics and students alike.

By slipping on VR headset, students attending the Beijing University of Chinese Medicine are now able to observe what was previously impossible to see—acupoints, meridians, and their regions of interest. These students can vividly view a wide variety of anatomical systems from a variety of angles, and most importantly, they can interact with a virtual avatar. This fantastic voyage inside the human body augments students' visual memory by creating an engaging and interactive environment that makes the experience novel and memorable.

Inside the classroom, teachers like Dr. Kai Cheng, professor of Beijing University of Chinese Medicine, explain what's going on, like how the acupoint BL54 is used to alleviate sciatica pain. During a needling simulation, students can see how the needle goes through the gluteus maximus to stimulate the sciatic nerve, and they observe the downstream dispersion through the sciatic nerve. Deeper penetration still will bring the needle to the perineum region and can relieve perineum-related diseases. Students can then take the needle into their own hands and practice this ancient skill of pain relief.

Even a few years back, it was hard to imagine how modern technology could find its way to assist with teachings that are over two millennia old and create a powerful learning tool in medical education. Dr. Shiu-Lin Tsai, assistant professor of emergency medicine at Columbia University Medical Center, uses auricular acupuncture to treat pediatric patients with acute pain. Her department is currently experimenting with VR to teach students, residents, and faculty members auricular battlefield acupuncture, a protocol she has implemented in the division of pediatric emergency medicine and has published on. Innovators like Dr. Tsai have recognized that VR has the power to provide a more engaging, immersive, and scalable learning tool for the next generation of medical professionals.

LEVELING UP IN THE CLASSROOM

While ancient Chinese acupuncture may not be at the top of your curriculum map for this year, it is clear what the incredible learning opportunities that this type of experience can provide. So many of our students today take vocational training in high school to learn skills that can help them in different careers. Sometimes those training programs are not offered in particular areas for reasons such as teacher availability, lack of resources, or transportation costs. Well, imagine if virtual reality was able to eliminate those issues by providing students with hands-on experiences in different fields to give them the training they need. This idea can really be applied to any school activity that requires experiential training, from science labs to equipment safety.

QUICK TIP

VR can provide opportunities to measurably improve learning outcomes. In Jesse's "Beyond the Classroom" story, he shared how a program called VirtualSpeech enabled him to better prepare for public speaking opportunities. Shannon Putman, an educator in Kentucky, did an experiment to see whether this kind of experience truly made a difference in her classroom. She had several students use VirtualSpeech to prepare for their talks while others prepared using traditional means. She found that all of the students who used VirtualSpeech scored high on a rubric she'd developed, while the ones who didn't use it almost universally fared much worse.

XR ABC TOOLBOX

| VR Blend | BodyMap |
| On Virtual Pins and Needles |
| Tags: *science, medicine, vocational* |

Platform: HTC Vive and Vive Pro, Oculus Rift, and Windows Mixed Reality

Tool: BodyMap is a VR app designed to help users understand human anatomy and their own bodies. You can move around the body to observe and comprehend anatomical structures with medically accurate human models based on actual MRI and CT scans.

Five Es (STEM)	Four Cs	ISTE Standards for Students
√ **Engage**	☐ Communication	☐ Empowered Learner
☐ Explore	√ **Critical Thinking**	☐ Digital Citizen
√ **Explain**	☐ Creativity	√ **Knowledge Constructor**
☐ Elaborate	☐ Collaboration	☐ Innovative Designer
√ **Evaluate**		☐ Computational Thinker
		☐ Creative Communicator
		☐ Global Collaborator

ISTE Standards for Educators	SAMR	QR Code for Additional Resources
☐ Learner	☐ Substitution	
√ **Leader**	√ **Augmentation**	
☐ Citizen	☐ Modification	
☐ Collaborator	☐ Redefinition	
☐ Designer		
√ **Facilitator**		
☐ Analyst		

Ready Learner Go!

In a world where all medical training has been done either with cadavers or in clinical trials, we are entering a time when medical practitioners' skill sets can constantly evolve in a way that lends itself toward positive growth. Think about how you would benefit as an educator from having the opportunity to test your instructional strategies with students prior to using them in your own classroom. How would that impact your practices?

Where Do We Go from Here?

The walls of the physical classroom present barriers that many educators do not have the capacity to break. The opportunity to engage learners in virtual reality allows us to bypass some of these physical barriers that limit learning. In a physical classroom space, studies of shapes, both 2-D and 3-D, are limited to what can be drawn on paper, crafted with blocks and other manipulatives, or constructed from paper, tape, and glue. While these methods of instructional engagement have certainly achieved the goal of teaching learners the fundamental knowledge of shapes, they have yet to prove innovative in approach or outcomes. Enter VR.

Learning the concepts of 2-D and 3-D shapes through an immersive experience alters both learning environment and the outcomes associated with the exploration of such knowledge. Sending students into a VR immersion where they can not only construct these shapes but also actually enter into the shapes and explore and analyze them from angles never before possible deepens the learning experience in entirely new ways. We are now teaching students to see, examine, evaluate, and iterate from perspectives that have never been previously accessible in a classroom — perspectives that aim toward the future.

Join the Conversation

1. How do VR Blend experiences inspire your instruction?
2. How do you engage your students with activities that are similar to the VR Blend activities in this chapter?
3. How can you use VR Blend work within your specific classroom?

Continue the conversation with your PLN by tweeting your responses using the hashtag #ReadyLearnerOne.

7
||||||||||||||||||||||||||||||||||||||||||||||||||||||||||||||||||
VR Create

Beyond the Classroom

I have played Minecraft and built a house or two, dug a hole, explored the Nether, etc. I have attempted to build structures in the popular gaming experience of Fortnite and ended up putting myself in a box that I had to destroy to get out of. Needless to say I have had some pretty unproductive experiences creating in VR. But then came Tilt Brush.

Tilt Brush, for those who are not familiar, is an artist palette and canvas in VR. It is a tool that allows the user to create multidimensional art, incorporate countless modalities of creation, and explore the final product from various perspectives. One of my first experiences with Tilt Brush left a lasting impression on me concerning the power of creating in a VR world. I stepped into Tilt Brush and immediately looked at my hands to gauge myself in this virtual space. I was pleased to see tools and an interactive palette that would allow me to create. I began to throw spatterings of colors and lines around and walked around them to see how they hung in this amazing space. The ability to easily walk into and around my creations was different than what I had seen in Minecraft and Fortnite—it was somehow more authentic. I created a stack of logs, piled like a pyramid, reminiscent of my camping days, and then added different colors. I'm no Bob Ross, but this was really working for me. In this visceral experience, it took my imagination very little effort to feel the heat of the flames I'd drawn and start looking for marshmallows to roast.

—Micah

Getting Started

PanoForm is a simple VR world creator. Use these directions to quickly create your own VR world.

1. Download a grid from https://panoform.com/.

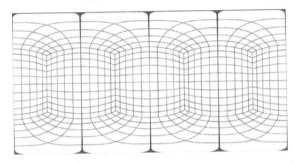

2. Print out the grid onto a letter-size sheet.
3. Color your own images (landscape, characters, environments, etc.).
4. Take a picture of your composition and crop to the corners of the grid.
5. If your device runs iOS, ensure Settings > Safari > Motion & Orientation Access is enabled.
6. Go to https://tool.panoform.com/.
7. Upload your composition from your phone library.
8. Tap the VR icon after the image loads.
9. Insert device into a Cardboard headset for the VR experience!

What is VR Create?

The power and magic of a truly great VR experience is undeniable. But what makes it a game changer for students is its ability to place them in a virtual environment and have them use their ideas and imaginations to demonstrate real learning and understanding.

Amber Klebanoff, an instructional innovation support specialist from Dobbs Ferry, New York, shared the following story:

> This year I've been working with a teacher who wanted to use Tour Creator after seeing just what Google Expeditions could do. She wanted her kids to create a tour of New York City from Holden Caulfield's point of view in *Catcher in the Rye*. I taught the teacher how

to use Tour Creator, and off she went. Students then created their own tours of New York City focusing on museums, Central Park, and other important points of interest. Students completed their projects and were able to see them with the Google Expeditions kit. Students narrated their tours, and their classmates were able to see in virtual reality some of the places Holden Caulfield traveled to in *Catcher in the Rye*.

James McCrary, a director of technology and cohost of the Virtual Reality podcast, shared:

> One of the experiences we created in an ELA class at my school recently involved students creating complex, variable storytelling in immersion technology. The students had to storyboard in one application, design assets in another, and compile all of them into CoSpaces, a VR world builder to share additional stories based on other stories they have read. Each turning point in the story had to have multiple variables so the audience could select how the story played out. And to boot, all of this was done on an iPad. During the project, these students were highly engaged. Not only with the process, but with each other. The dedication to create their authentic story and have the audience experience it in such a meaningful way was inspiring. And on the topic of standards, the students went well beyond the targeted standards and completed the project in the same amount of time typically allocated for instructing the standards in the traditional method. Moreover, the amount of collaboration and critical thinking involved with this project was off the charts and not really possible without the integration of virtual reality as a vehicle for storytelling.

Using virtual reality as a tool for consumption provides incredibly rich opportunities to experience new worlds, environments, and experiences. But under the VR Create aspect of the XR ABC framework, VR goes beyond that to allow for world creation. Students become owners, developing the products of their learning as opposed to just experiencing them, which brings a deeper level of connection and understanding for learners.

Pop-Culture Connection

While our company name has been clearly influenced by the book and movie *Ready Player One* and its vision of virtual reality through the world created

within its OASIS, it would be hard to have a conversation about virtual reality in the movies without discussing the 1999 classic *The Matrix*. In one of the greatest years in cinematic history, we were treated to a vision for what a mass-populated virtual world could look like. Our protagonist, Keanu Reeves's character, finds out (SPOILER ALERT) that the world he's been living in is just a virtual simulation and that in reality, most people are connected to wires and living in this simulation as well — also, they are sleeping in some kind of goo.

Apart from the goo, think about how as they exist within this virtual world, people live out their lives and existences by creating experiences for themselves just as we do in real life. That is exactly the kind of thing we expect to happen in a VR Create experience. Using the "powers" granted by the creators of a VR experience, users can make content that's not present by default. So after this, "There is no turning back. You take the blue pill — the story ends, you wake up in your bed and believe whatever you want to believe. You take the red pill — you stay in Wonderland, and I show you how deep the rabbit hole goes." Which will it be?

CLASSROOM CHRONICLES
CREATION THROUGH EXPLORATION
STEVE ISAACS

In May of 2014, I began exploring the possibility of participating in research on virtual reality in the classroom, starting with foundry10, an educational-research foundation based in Seattle. I had worked with foundry10 previously and I was a fan based on their focus on exploring nontraditional approaches to learning. Their approach to the VR project was for educators to apply and provide their ideas of how they would like to incorporate VR in their work. The research would be modeled around the ideas that were accepted. Content creation in VR was the area I wanted to focus on. I knew very little about virtual reality at the time, but I saw this as an incredible opportunity for students to get involved with cutting-edge technology and, while there was not much content available, focus on learning to create content (whatever that might look like).

It seemed important for students to experience VR incrementally before diving into the deep end in terms of content creation. We explored and explored and explored some more. Students wrote in-depth reviews of VR content (you can find many of their reviews at http://bit.ly/VRreviews). There's a lot of talk about moving past the wow factor when it comes to technology, but I do believe it is often that very "wow" that inspires and informs us. We quickly realized that there was some really cool VR content and some really poorly executed VR content. It can be frustrating that much of the commercially released content feels much more like a prototype than an experience that truly leverages what is possible with this remarkable technology. This led me to think that we are still in the infancy of this rapidly growing industry. This realization made me very excited about the possibilities regarding content-creation opportunities for students. Students could be creating content from the inception of the technology.

Failure often leads to opportunity. The newness of the tech provided great opportunities to explore, experiment, and make many mistakes. My initial thought was that Unity (a cross-platform game engine) would be a great tool for student-created VR content. We learned many lessons working with Unity. Our first lesson was that there's a pretty steep learning curve. I work with middle school students, and I've spoken with other educators who have had success with Unity. Many share a similar sentiment of it being quite challenging. Developmentally, I think high school is probably the sweet spot for starting to learn Unity. When working with middle-school students, I've learned several times in my career, it's great when the on-ramp to a new technology is reasonable and students can start creating meaningful content early on. This was not the case with Unity. Students would spend a large amount of time getting a few objects into Unity and then have to transfer their files to the computer with the HTC Vive or Oculus Rift to test their build. From a work-flow standpoint, this was pretty cumbersome. My class is choice based, so I was certainly open to students experimenting with Unity, and some were more successful than others. One of the best experiences was when I was able to connect a professional Unity game developer with one group of students as a mentor. This team was able to communicate directly with the developer; as a result, the students were highly motivated and willing to take on much of the learning outside of class. When the course ended, I bid these students farewell as they were moving on to high school, but in the back of my head, I was hoping to create other opportunities for them. Whenever I find a group of students who find their passion and embrace learning, I want to find a way to nurture that passion.

As I reflected on my initial experiences with Unity, it occurred to me that I really wanted to find ways for students to develop content for VR without expecting them to jump in the deep end. I have been using Minecraft extensively in my game-development classes for the past six years. Minecraft can be played in VR using the Oculus Rift or Windows Mixed Reality. We have both. I was using Minecraft often as a sample VR experience for my students, but it took me a while to realize the potential for creating content for VR in Minecraft. Sometimes we can't see the forest through the trees.

Six years ago when I started using Minecraft, I wasn't convinced that it was the right tool for game design. I did know that students *loved* the game and couldn't stop talking about it; I had to find a way to incorporate it into my classes. I quickly saw that Minecraft is in fact a tremendous game-design platform. Once I reframed my thinking I likewise came to realize what a great tool it is as an entry point for creating content for virtual reality. I started to create activities that allowed students to create content in Minecraft specifically to be experienced in VR. My students quickly started to make observations about what makes content work or not work for VR.

They began to realize that a regular Minecraft world often involved small passageways or narrow staircases for the player to go through, and in virtual reality this can make a player claustrophobic or otherwise uncomfortable. Students started to collaborate in a unique way because of the medium. One student would be in the VR headset while a partner was in Minecraft not in VR. They were communicating and modifying their world in real time based on feedback from their VR partner. It led to great conversations about creating content for virtual reality because it made so much sense in context.

Since the first team took on this project, many have followed suit, and they are creating unique experiences including games and amusement parks (particularly roller coasters). One team even re-created a part of New York City where the player could stand on an observation deck on top of the Empire State Building to view the city skyline. We always talk about meeting kids where they are, and using Minecraft in this way allowed me to do just that while still meeting the learning outcome of creating content for virtual reality.

LEVELING UP IN THE CLASSROOM

There are many ways to leverage Minecraft in the classroom for content creation. These creation experiences can be aligned with a plethora of content areas where students design in a problem-based learning experience. For example, in a social-studies class where students are studying ancient civilizations and the layout of society, a challenge could be to design an irrigation system or a housing area taking into consideration the natural resources of the area.

Taking the concept of putting students in the driver's seat of creation and development, Steve Isaacs shares this parting thought:

> I am currently working on a grant with Verizon and Games for Change. We will be running twenty XR hackathons across the country to work with students in underserved areas. The theme of the hackathons will involve what's possible with XR and 5G technology. Students will have an opportunity to work with a variety of tools including Minecraft, CoSpacesEDU, Windows Mixed Reality, virtual reality, and augmented reality with the MERGE Cube. It will be exciting to see what students prototype and develop to explore what will be possible when 5G technology and extended reality meet.

QUICK TIP

How can you engage the entire class in VR when only one student is participating in an experience? You can cast or stream what the user sees in their VR goggles to the rest of the class, but that doesn't always do the experience justice. A 2019 episode of *The Tonight Show with Jimmy Fallon* featured a segment with Jimmy and Brie Larson playing Beat Saber (as seen here: http://bit.ly/latenightbeatsaber) that got people all over the country excited. The cool part was that while they were wearing their VR headsets viewers could still see the entire experience happening right in front of them. For more information on how you can create this kind of experience with a green screen, check out the book resources for *Reality Bytes* at http://readylearner.one.

XR ABC TOOLBOX

VR Create	Minecraft and Unity
Creation through Exploration
Tags: unity, minecraft, creation

Platform: PC, Mac, Oculus Rift, HTC Vive, and Windows Mixed Reality

Tool: Minecraft and Unity can be used as content-creation tools.

Five Es (STEM)	Four Cs	ISTE Standards for Students
√ **Engage**	√ **Communication**	☐ Empowered Learner
☐ Explore	√ **Critical Thinking**	☐ Digital Citizen
☐ Explain	√ **Creativity**	☐ Knowledge Constructor
√ **Elaborate**	√ **Collaboration**	√ **Innovative Designer**
☐ Evaluate		√ **Computational Thinker**
		√ **Creative Communicator**
		√ **Global Collaborator**

ISTE Standards for Educators	SAMR	QR Code for Additional Resources
☐ Learner	☐ Substitution	
√ **Leader**	☐ Augmentation	
☐ Citizen	☐ Modification	
☐ Collaborator	√ **Redefinition**	
☐ Designer		
√ **Facilitator**		
√ **Analyst**		

Ready Learner Go!

What are your biggest challenges when embracing a tool like Minecraft or Unity in your classroom? For most educators, it is lack of familiarity and, thus, confidence and comfort with the tool. Challenge yourself to watch YouTube video tutorials, explore blog posts, and jump into these tools to build a foundation for yourself so that you can be more confident in presenting them to your students.

CLASSROOM CHRONICLES
WHO TELLS YOUR STORY?
BRIAN COSTELLO

I am a storyteller. Throughout my teaching career, I have enjoyed telling stories and helping my students find their own stories to tell. I hadn't really thought about using virtual or augmented reality for storytelling when I first started sharing them with my students. We explored places and things like viruses, bacteria, and more. But we were consumers in a world waiting to be created. The virtual field trips and the 360° models were great and useful, but I knew the novelty would wear off soon. I was desperately seeking an opportunity for my kids to display their knowledge through something they could view in either virtual or augmented reality.

There were a few options at the time, but in truth, I needed something easy. I was working as a technology-integration teacher, so I could only take small periods of time with my middle-school classes. I started to feel as though the novelty of XR was going to mean it would only be used on a single occasion each year. Until I found CoSpaces. CoSpaces was easy to use, it had plenty of possibilities, and my kids could use it on the computer, through a phone screen, or even in virtual reality. But what to do with it?

Creating in virtual reality and augmented reality has become a common occurrence in my classrooms over the past few years, but the best ideas and lessons have been spurred from the first two times I gave VR creation to my students and let them build. While their creations were interesting and a great way to demonstrate their understanding, it wasn't their content that piqued my interest, it was something more.

The first class that created in virtual reality did so by chance. I was assigned to an English class that was taking practice tests. Fortunately, they finished early. With about twenty minutes left in the period, the teacher said to me, "Is there anything you want to do with them?" So, I took the chance. I put them on CoSpaces and gave them a three-minute crash course. They spent the next fifteen minutes demonstrating an understanding of figurative language. It wasn't that they created figurative-language scenes that impressed me, but that in the fifteen minutes we had, many of them told intriguing stories while demonstrating what they knew. Storytelling to demonstrate knowledge was interesting for me, for them, and in general. That storytelling made perfect sense in an English class.

LEVELING UP IN THE CLASSROOM

In Brian's next CoSpaces assignment, he reached out to a teacher that was typically willing to let him try new things with her class. She gave him three classes to have students build some sort of chain reaction based on the concept of a Rube Goldberg machine. Brian gave the students only a handful of constraints for the assignment after a short tutorial. Students had to create a series of small events that would launch a rocket. It needed to have at least three events in the reaction. Otherwise, he allowed them the freedom to create. What happened over the next two class periods was incredible. Their projects were more than just a series of chain reactions, they were stories. Almost all of the students created some sort of story about how or why the rocket was being launched. Rather than just build the chain reaction, these new creators had taken it upon themselves to use storytelling in VR to express themselves.

QUICK TIP

One of the best ways to improve students' experiences of the incorporation of VR and AR into your teaching is to consistently provide opportunities for students to give feedback. This can be as simple as providing an online form or comment area to collect feedback. Feedback like this can help you refine your lesson plans to leverage each particular experience.

When Micah showed his class the Anne Frank House VR experience mentioned at the end of the VR Absorb chapter, one of the students commented that "the Anne Frank House VR experience helped me understand Anne Frank's story because it allowed me to visualize what was happening to her better. It showed how cramped the rooms were that Anne Frank was living in and why they had to be very cautious and quiet because the floors were made out of creaky wood and the only thing keeping them hidden was a bookshelf on hinges. The experience helped me to put things into perspective and understand what Anne was going through better."

XR ABC TOOLBOX

VR Create | CoSpaces
<u>Who Tells Your Story?</u>
Tags: storytelling, language arts

Platform: Internet browser, iOS and Android devices

Tool: CoSpaces is a tool that enables students and teachers to easily build their own 3-D creations, animate them with code, and explore them in virtual or augmented reality.

Five Es (STEM)	Four Cs	ISTE Standards for Students
√ **Engage**	√ **Communication**	☐ Empowered Learner
☐ Explore	√ **Critical Thinking**	☐ Digital Citizen
☐ Explain	√ **Creativity**	☐ Knowledge Constructor
☐ Elaborate	√ **Collaboration**	√ **Innovative Designer**
☐ Evaluate		☐ Computational Thinker
		☐ Creative Communicator
		☐ Global Collaborator

ISTE Standards for Educators	SAMR	QR Code for Additional Resources
☐ Learner	☐ Substitution	
☐ Leader	☐ Augmentation	
☐ Citizen	☐ Modification	
☐ Collaborator	√ **Redefinition**	
☐ Designer		
√ **Facilitator**		
☐ Analyst		

Ready Learner Go!

On a computer:

1. Go to CoSpaces.io and sign up for a free account.
2. Create your first Space in a 3D Environment.
3. Click "environment" and then "edit" to select a setting.
4. Click "library" and drag a few images and characters into your Environment.
5. Click "play" in the top right to see your world in VR.

On an iOS or Android device:

1. Download the CoSpaces app.
2. Log in with the same credentials you used on your computer.
3. Select your Space and click "play." You will now have the option to view it with VR goggles (see icon).

Note: In the app, you can also choose AR to view your images and characters on a flat surface.

CLASSROOM CHRONICLES
BUILDING BLOCKS IN SUSTAINABILITY
MATT GOTTILLA

In my eighth-grade STEAM (science, technology, engineering, arts, and math) class, one of the major areas of focus is sustainability. The culmination of our exploration of sustainability is a project where students collaborate in small groups to design their own self-sustaining communities. Previously, students created 3-D models of their communities using materials like Legos, cardboard, and paper. This year, our district completed a new STEAM lab, housing three VR setups. Immediately, I began brainstorming and researching ways for students to become content creators in VR and to incorporate this new technology in meaningful ways. The self-sustaining community project felt like the perfect opportunity to utilize virtual reality in a way that met both of these goals and significantly enhanced the student experience.

The first challenge was finding a suitable program the students could use to create their communities. While I had worked with students to create 3-D models in the past using programs like Tinkercad, I really wanted to afford students the opportunity to design in virtual reality. After some searching, I came across Google Blocks. After viewing the trailer for the program and trying it out myself, I was convinced it would be the right tool for the job. Blocks would allow students to create in VR and to do so in an intuitive way.

After some reimagining of the work flow for the project, it was time to dive in. We started out by outlining our goals. Students would need to design a community that was self-sustaining in terms of energy production, food production, and waste management. Their community would have access to both a lake and a river. They would be allotted funding for twenty buildings. Ultimately, they would produce a 3-D model of their community that they would use to take their classmates on a virtual tour.

After discussing the requirements and constraints, groups met for the first time to start planning their building selections. They needed to decide what essentials they should include as well as what other buildings they wanted to spend on. Students came into this project with a strong understanding of the pros and cons of various energy sources, and one of the first items groups settled on was how they wanted to power their communities. From there, students enumerated the remaining necessities and quickly began giving their communities unique spins with their remaining building selections.

Next, it was time for students to plan the layout of their communities. We discussed the choices they would be making, such as where to locate the residential areas, what structures it made sense to have near each other, and how transportation throughout their community would look. Students did additional research, learning about topics like urban agriculture and pedestrian-friendly roads. They drew inspiration from existing self-sustaining community designs as well as intelligent engineering and design from cities around the world. Students then drafted 2-D scale maps of their communities, incorporating the buildings, transportation, and public spaces they had decided on.

Finally, it was time to get students into virtual reality. After learning the basics of Google Blocks, students began bringing their communities to life. One useful feature of Blocks is the ability to import reference images. By photographing students' 2-D maps, I was able to bring them into the virtual environment so that students could refer to them as they began creating their communities. Students could even move and enlarge the maps, allowing them to position them however was most helpful for them. Some students even elected to lay their map flat and build up from it vertically, overlaying their structures exactly where they had drawn them out by hand.

Over the course of the next month, the students' creations took shape. The beginnings of a city with solar farms on its outskirts and a bustling downtown could be seen on one screen, while another community powered by wind turbines and boasting a riverfront residential area was visible on another. Bike-friendly arrangements and an emphasis on public transportation could be found in many of the virtual spaces. Students were eager to hop into their communities each day, ready to add a school or farm, or to improve the aesthetics of some of their existing buildings. When all of the structures and roadways were complete, several groups continued to improve upon their communities by developing their public spaces in more detail, planting gardens and trees, or including sculptures and artwork. After several weeks of energetic development, our communities were ready to be shared.

We gathered around one of the VR setups as a student from the presenting group donned the headset. On the flat screen above her head, the class could see her community. Her group members proceeded to describe their design as the student moved around or dragged the virtual landscape to bring the areas in question into closer view. After completing this virtual tour for the class, we invited any interested students to put on the VR headset and experience the community for themselves. All groups showcased their work in this way, capping off a momentous undertaking in an engaging experience where students could truly appreciate their classmates' creations.

LEVELING UP IN THE CLASSROOM

Google Blocks is an intuitive creation tool for VR. It encourages students to design and develop prototypes aligned with project-based learning. Consider using Google Blocks creation tools in a middle-school social-studies class that is studying the architecture of ancient amphitheaters. Students can design an amphitheater, employing the architectural rules applied by the ancient Greeks, and build a prototype in Google Blocks. Students can then take peers on a tour of their design and compare and contrast it to other amphitheaters of other cultures and civilizations. Take it one step further and export the file to be printed on a 3-D printer.

XR ABC TOOLBOX

VR Create | Google Blocks
Building Blocks in Sustainability
Tags: STEAM, architecture, science

Platform: HTC Vive or Oculus Rift
Tool: Google Blocks is a tool that allows users to easily create three-dimensional models in virtual reality regardless of their experience level.

Five Es (STEM)	Four Cs	ISTE Standards for Students
√ **Engage**	√ **Communication**	☐ Empowered Learner
☐ Explore	√ **Critical Thinking**	☐ Digital Citizen
√ **Explain**	√ **Creativity**	☐ Knowledge Constructor
√ **Elaborate**	√ **Collaboration**	√ **Innovative Designer**
☐ Evaluate		☐ Computational Thinker
		√ **Creative Communicator**
		☐ Global Collaborator

ISTE Standards for Educators	SAMR	QR Code for Additional Resources
☐ Learner	☐ Substitution	
√ **Leader**	☐ Augmentation	
☐ Citizen	☐ Modification	
☐ Collaborator	√ **Redefinition**	
☐ Designer		
√ **Facilitator**		
☐ Analyst		

Ready Learner Go!
Check out these creations by students using Google Blocks:
- bit.ly/LittleZebraFish
- bit.ly/UpHouseBalloons
- bit.ly/HomeBlocksHome

Consider how you can use Google Blocks to engage your learners.

Where Do We Go from Here?

In an interview with Eugene Belyaev, founder of CoSpaces, we learned a great deal about how this Munich-based company has responsively grown a successful tool for education. Their story lends insight into how user testing and user experience can and should heavily influence the direction emergent technology solutions will take.

Development for CoSpaces, originally called Coaching Spaces, began in 2012 with a 2014 release. CoSpaces was created and developed for a very small market as a tool for helping people in therapy and counseling. The psychologists and coaches Eugene had been developing for were not tech savvy, so user testing was very important. During the development phases Eugene would regularly put users into the experiences and ask them for feedback. Psychologists and coaches (professional counselors) started to use CoSpaces to work with patients in a virtual space. These 3-D virtual environments were leveraged by desktop computers since VR wasn't widespread at the time. Clients in sessions would use CoSpaces for mapping out issues and concerns. They would use a simple graphics library full of colorful shapes and symbols to represent issues and concerns that they had. Originally, male and female figures were included in the library but without faces. This collaborative online environment allowed multiple users to have a virtual space to create and engage in.

Google Cardboard started to make VR more accessible, so Eugene explored using it with his CoSpaces app. Immediately, he went about his usual user testing work to refine the product. With this new app psychologists could "fly" into the perspectives of the people they were working with, providing amazing experiences for empathy. The psychologists reported that they were having breakthroughs by helping their clients go into the perspectives of others with the issues and concerns that they were exploring. Eugene found real success in an extremely small market.

While in middle school, Eugene's daughter loved to play and create using Minecraft and the Sims. One day she saw Eugene's CoSpaces app and said, "I want to try it!" She started to build scenes, houses with rooms, and playgrounds. She began to model characters, and by using the shapes available, she made faces on the characters. Watching his daughter play in his product meant for another type of user led to Eugene's efforts to roll out the version of CoSpaces more of us are familiar with.

Eugene was experienced in building tools for non–tech savvy users, so CoSpaces (2016) was prototyped for children and nonspecific users. Education was not initially a target audience. However, Eugene noticed large groups of people from the same unique email domain were signing up for

CoSpaces accounts . . . it was schools. From then forward CoSpaces grew into a more school-friendly app, with Eugene constantly working to keep it at the cutting edge.

Join the Conversation

1. What current instructional strategies can you substitute with a VR Create lesson?
2. How can VR Create activities help you redefine your instruction?
3. In what ways can VR Create inspire student productivity?

Continue the conversation with your PLN by tweeting your responses using the hashtag #ReadyLearnerOne.

8

Perspectives from the Developer Side

An Educator's Worldview

As educators, we naturally see XR technologies through our teacher lens. We look for the instructional good in every tool and resource. We think about the impact that it will have on the overall student experience. We examine how our learning outcomes will be impacted by the role that technology will play in our classrooms and with our students. We ideate on how we can assess for growth as a result of student use. We are educators. It's what we do.

However, we often don't take time to examine the perspectives and intended outcomes of the developers of the tools of our trade. As XR technologies are becoming increasingly prevalent in education today, it is the responsibility of developers in the realm to be cognizant of how education evolves and the needs of the students whom the technology serves. This chapter explores the role of XR technology in education through the perspective of one of these developers, Lorenzo Vallone, who has a vision for using XR to globally impact learning in a positive, meaningful, and purposeful way. Here's his story.

A Vision of XR Learning — Lorenzo Vallone

We're at the dawn of an incredible transformation in education. The computing power of technological innovations continues to grow exponentially. Technologies like XR, artificial intelligence (AI), cloud computing, robotics, and the Internet of Things are converging on the education industry and beginning to force the reevaluation of long-held ideas and methodologies. A multitude of technologies, from e-learning to video communications to learning-management solutions to smartboards, have impacted classrooms worldwide. But I believe these technological successes will pale in comparison to what is ahead of us.

Xennial Digital was one of the pioneers in the use of VR for K–12 STEM learning. We leveraged early versions of the HTC Vive and Oculus Rift and predicted that schools all over the world would embrace this technology due to its immersive power, relative low cost, and ease of use. As with most predictions, we were somewhat right, mostly wrong, and way too early, but we persist and persevere like many others in our emerging industry.

On the one hand, we have been inspired by the fact that most students exposed to our immersive learning experiences have embraced them with open arms. We have also been fortunate to find many visionaries and leaders among the administrators, teachers, and technologists in private and public schools who have taken leaps of faith to bring these solutions one step closer to all students.

But the factors working against widespread adoption of new technology in K–12 are massive. The resistance to taking risks and investing money, time, and teacher training in cutting-edge technology is strong. The good news, for those of us that see this challenge as a pathway to inevitable change, is that change is, in fact, inevitable. At some point in the very near future, as XR devices and content continue to mature and converge with powerful 5G cloud and artificial intelligence technology, the concept of not using XR in learning will be unimaginable.

The reason is quite simple: XR breaks down the constraining walls of the three-dimensional physical environment, which no other technology that has emerged to date has been able to do.

Photorealistic, highly interactive, virtual replicas of real-world environments of all types — from the Library of Congress to the most advanced engineering labs on earth to your local elementary school — will become available to any student at any time from anywhere in the world. When users can be immersed in a near-identical virtual recreation of a physical environment with a near-zero cost to operate and accessible to any student with a $400 headset, the value of physical space drops exponentially.

Students from all over the world will converge in these virtual places to work together, to learn, and to solve complex real-world challenges. AI will precisely measure their individual learning progress and adapt their learning experience with more and more challenging work that is tailored to their unique interests and learning styles. The very best teachers from all over the world will join in the virtual environments, providing guidance, mentorship, and knowledge. Incredibly powerful lightweight headsets coupled with haptic gloves and suits and other multisensory devices will reproduce real-world physical experiences within the virtual learning environments. And all this happens at massive scale, with the highest level of security, with blockchain tracking all the data capture, and at a tiny fraction of the cost of maintaining today's physical school infrastructure. This may sound like science fiction — something out of *Ready Player One* — but the reality is that the technology to do all of it exists today, and it's getting exponentially faster, cheaper, and more powerful.

Virtual reality experiences that approximate the real world break the limitations imposed by older forms of learning content such as videos, computer animations, and textbooks, and they put the students in a place where they are truly free to focus on the experience and to practice as if they were in the real world but without risk and without cost.

XR learning makes sense for many reasons:

1. Significant reduction in the cost of physical labs and experiments
2. Corresponding reduction in need for physical space
3. Opportunity to repeat labs, experiments, and simulations repeatedly with near-zero incremental cost
4. Free up teacher time over traditional labs
5. Access to these immersive experiences on devices that cost less than $400
6. Near-zero risk to perform labs and simulations
7. Significant increase in the amount of performance data available
8. Increased focus and engagement by students
9. Increased learning retention
10. Democratization of these technologies for anyone, anywhere in the world
11. Increase in collaborative learning by enabling students and teachers from anywhere in the world to work together in virtual experiences
12. Access to previously impossible, dangerous, or prohibitively expensive experiences

About XD Learning

XD Learning is a VR solution that encompasses a secure, cloud-based platform along with a growing library of STEM learning titles covering areas of biology, physics, chemistry, anatomy, and more. The original vision was to leverage the power of virtual reality to provide students with a powerful, engaging, and immersive way of exploring and learning about complex science concepts. These multisensory, kinesthetic learning experiences immerse students in a highly realistic virtual world and enable them to learn science concepts through repeated practice without risk or cost.

For example, to learn about the Doppler effect, students find themselves in a photorealistic train station, able to control a train moving between sixty and three hundred miles per hour. The student can change the frequency of the whistle and visualize the Doppler effect as the train cruises. The accurate, real-time formulas on a big board in the station adapt as the train moves. To learn about fungi, students find themselves walking through a rich forest with a lake they can swim in and with deer, butterflies, and the sounds of birds around them. As they discover various types of fungi, they can shrink themselves to a microscopic level to experience, from the inside out, how the fungi feed and reproduce. To learn about gravity, friction, and energy, students are transported to a massive indoor skate park with twenty-foot skate ramps and virtual skaters rushing by. The student is able to control the gravity, friction, and mass of a skater and see at full speed and in slow motion how energy is transferred as the skater moves up and down the ramps.

After launching the pilot platform and onboarding several schools, we validated something remarkable that we had already begun to understand anecdotally in the schools that were using the solution. In a research study conducted at Columbia University,[1] a PhD candidate named Elliot Hu-Au compared the learning efficacy of using video, 2-D simulation, and XD Learning with a group of fifty graduate students. What emerged was the discovery that by using VR, subjects reported a 77 percent higher motivation to learn more and an 85 percent increase in interest in the subject.

Our team had a firsthand experience with this early on that was pivotal to cementing our faith and dedication to the power of XR Learning. My cofounder and Xennial Digital's CEO, Douglas Fajardo, is originally from Guatemala and has a deep love for his beautiful country and its people. Xennial Digital has worked with The Nature Conservancy and rural farmers in Guatemala to launch a learning experience that uses VR on Oculus Go headsets to teach farmers how to implement sustainable farming practices in light of the impact of climate change on their lands.

Douglas has also organized an opportunity for Xennial Digital to donate HTC Vive VR hardware and our VR learning platform to a school located almost four hours outside of Guatemala City. This small rural school had only recently received internet access thanks to a local nonprofit. The Xennial Digital team traveled to Guatemala and installed the HTC Vive hardware and laptop at the school. We were thrilled to see how quickly the teacher and students embraced and mastered all the experiences in the XD Learning platform. They installed other solutions such as Google Earth and Tilt Brush and began to explore the world in ways they could not have previously imagined. On its own merit, this is a remarkable illustration of how a small dose of technology could have a profound impact on the lives of so many young students. But this incredible story had only just begun.

A month later we received a video. A small group of seventh- and eighth-grade students from the school, along with their teacher, had taken the VR gear apart and loaded it onto a bus for an hour-long ride to an even more remote village. This particular village did not have electricity except for a tiny community center. Most of the homes used kerosene or candles for light, which resulted in pollution and fires. The video we received illustrated how the students had set up the VR gear in the community center after receiving a donation of small circuit boards, batteries, and LED lights.

The students then used one of the XD Learning VR experiences on electrical circuits to teach the adults how to wire the circuit board to the battery and to the light bulb so that they could bring this source of light to their homes.

In one month, these motivated students in rural Guatemala had used XD Learning to become innovators and teachers themselves; in doing so they brought light to where there was once darkness. Xennial Digital was proud to have been named Guatemala's most innovative company in 2018 as a result.

And yet the value of XR learning only begins with increased student engagement. There are other more pragmatic advantages. First, the cost and time to build biology, chemistry, or physics labs in schools is astronomical. Now for a small fraction of the cost, schools can provide students with a wide range of science lab experiences using virtual reality. In addition, virtual reality provides a distraction-free environment. Unlike the web, where students can get easily distracted by the noise of a web page, once you are in a virtual reality experience, there is little else to do but focus on the task at hand. Next, the level of learning retention using virtual reality is exponentially greater than with video- or audio-based learning content. Professor Edgar Dale in his work on the cone of experience in 1969 noted that we retain 10 percent of what we read, 20 percent of what we hear, and 90 percent of what we do.[2] Of course, I doubt that Dr. Dale envisioned a Magic Leap or Oculus Quest on every student's head, but his findings apply in a profound way to the power of XR learning, since XR is as close to doing as we can get short of the physical experience.

Building XR Learning Experiences Collaboratively

I was visiting a partner high school in South Florida that was working with Xennial Digital to develop a new experience for the platform, when I noticed two tenth-grade students working in the VR lab, each wearing individual VR headsets. At first it was not clear what they were doing, but as I approached, I could see on the large screens connected to the HTC Vive headsets that they were inside a new XD Learning experience that was not even 50 percent completed at that point and far from being launched. It was truly an early beta release.

As I watched what they were doing, I realized that they were actually in the same VR experience together, each represented as robot avatars. The students could see each other's avatar as it moved within the experience and they were able to talk to one another from within the experience as well.

Before I had time to understand how these students were able to gain access to an early beta release of one of our experiences, I heard other voices coming from within the experience and noticed that there were additional avatars with the students. These voices were familiar. They turned out to be our lead architect and lead creative designer from our team in Colombia along with a senior project manager from our Miami office.

As I watched in awe, the two students offered ideas and guidance related to the experience to our team of highly trained developers and project managers. They were collaborating together in the most natural way imaginable, designing the experience from the inside out. It was a surreal moment for me, watching these five people located in physically disparate places working together inside the same VR experience to build the very experience they were in. But the most inspiring realization for me was that the very people who were the ultimate customers of these experiences — the students — were at the center of the software-development process with us.

I had witnessed the organic creation of a new model of work where students and teachers could collaborate with expert product designers and software developers to produce VR learning experiences faster, with greater quality, and more aligned to the needs of the end customer.

As I walked away, I began to wonder if and how this model could be replicated and scaled. As I thought through the opportunity, the benefits to both sides — developers and educators — became extremely clear. Utilizing a team of dedicated students who could provide research, creative ideas, content writing, project coordination, and quality assurance was an opportunity to create higher-quality experiences more rapidly. This could impact Xennial Digital's commercial success, and in the process, the students would have the opportunity to learn new skills from our team of experienced product designers, project managers, 3-D artists, and software developers. These skills could potentially shape the future of their educations and careers. And they would be part of a team producing VR learning experiences that would feature their names as producers in the credits, outlive their time in school, and serve to help thousands of other students learn key STEM concepts. It was truly a win, win, win.

Of course, achieving this utopian state was not going to be without challenges and pitfalls along the way. When I was first pitched the idea internally it fell hard on its face. Valid questions were raised about bandwidth within our teams, questions of resources, cost, time, potential delays, and quality control. But after significant deliberation, it was ultimately agreed that the benefits could outweigh the cost and risk. It was something to at least try — if we could find the right opportunity.

And as often happens in these situations, the universe answered just a few weeks later. I had been introduced to Christine Lion-Bailey and Steve Isaacs through Grant Hagen at ByteSpeed, an amazing VR-hardware distribution partner. I was able to pitch them the idea over the phone, and they were thrilled to be part of the experiment. Shortly thereafter, ten students ranging from seventh to ninth grade were recruited from two schools to work on the project. This diverse group of amazing students, led by their dedicated teachers, began to have regular weekly meetings with Xennial's team to figure out how to upgrade the XD Learning VR Bat Cave experience. The students rose to the challenge from day one. Some gravitated to the technical side, some to the creative, and some to the project management. It was as close to the utopian dream as we could have achieved in the just ten weeks available.

The success of the program cannot be understated. However, there were two key lessons. First, a twelve- or twenty-four-week timeline would be more suitable, especially for younger students, to complete a complex project such as VR learning. Secondly, because our team was effectively operating on a pro bono basis, distractions from client projects interfered with the planned schedule. As we seek to further refine and formalize this incredible collaborative software-development process, there are a few key considerations. First, it's important to raise the necessary funds required to make this type of program work on a formal scale. This will enable Xennial Digital to dedicate a design and development team to the project for the duration of the program. And secondly, we would seek to offer the teacher and students a comprehensive introductory technical training in development platforms such as Unity or Unreal. Lastly, we would seek to formalize the program management process to ensure that the final product is built, tested, and delivered.

Despite the minor challenges, setbacks, and lessons learned, the experience proved to us without a shadow of a doubt that the formula has merit: bright, motivated students plus inspired, dedicated teachers plus industry experts with a reason for caring equals amazing outcomes!

Conclusion

Exponential technology is all around us and is impacting nearly every area of how we live and work. XR is a technology with the power to transform education like no other. With the ability to transform how students learn challenging concepts more efficiently combined with the ability to immerse students in virtual, lifelike spaces without risk or incremental cost, the technology offers tremendous opportunity for the future of learning.

For schools, administrators, and teachers, the challenges are twofold: First is how to inspire the millions of creative-minded, fearless future product developers, engineers, computer scientists, doctors, technicians, and so many more that will create the future we envision. At the same time, how will educational systems adapt in an age where the power of XR converging with other exponential technologies such as 5G and AI will transform what learning means and how it is delivered to students?

The role of the teacher will be absolutely central to managing this transformation. Teachers will need to embrace and evangelize not just XR learning but all of these new exponential technologies while at the same time using these technologies to inspire students.

9

A Peek into the Future

The Secret Sauce: Funding

More than likely there was a point in this book where you stopped and asked yourself, "How am I ever going to get this technology purchased in my school/district?" While it is true that providing students, and teachers, with access to high-end VR equipment is quite costly, it is also a very attainable ambition should one choose to embark on that journey.

There are numerous opportunities to acquire funding for XR technologies in the learning environment. Grants are among the most common. When writing a grant to support the adoption of XR technologies, we must first consider the impact that technology will have on the student experience. The stories in this book make it quite clear that the technology is an ingredient in incredible learning experiences resulting in global awareness and fostering empathy, critical thinking, creative outlets, decision-making processes, advocacy for self and others, citizenship, and more. While XR technology is not required to teach these things, it is a vehicle that allows a perspective unlike any other. When crafting a grant application to support adoption of XR technology, consider incorporating these valuable learning outcomes to attract the grant evaluator's support. For a list of specific grant opportunities, outside of your own community grants, please visit the Ready Learner One website at http://readylearner.one. On our site, you will find a library of grant opportunities with supporting points of contact for each.

So now that you know that you have the ability to fund these types of technologies in your school, what does it look like for the future?

The Future of Work:
The Role of Emergent Technology

We know that we must be preparing students for their futures. The words "their future" are used here purposefully in lieu of the usual "the future" — as educators, we are not tasked with generically preparing students for the future. We are tasked with preparing students for a future that is their own to embrace, define, and adventure throughout. We must look at each student individually and provide them with learning opportunities that will help them to define themselves, their characteristics, strengths, weaknesses, passions, and talents so that they can carve their own path into the vast unknown that we refer to as the future.

Even though we may not know exactly what the future holds, history has shown that we can do a pretty good job of guessing what it might look like. *Dick Tracy* in 1931 predicted smart watches. *The Jetsons* predicted robot vacuums (YES!) and flying cars (drone versions are already in testing).[1] And, of course, *Back to the Future* predicted augmented reality, wearable tech, and hoverboards. With that in mind, how do we prepare students to have the skills needed to thrive regardless of the innovations in technology that will happen?

The Future of Work: Soft Skills

In a world where innovation is happening faster than we can learn and master things, we need to identify the skills that will best serve students as they prepare for their future. As artificial intelligence and bots continue to grow in popularity when it comes to effectively (both in terms of cost and consistency) completing task-based work, we need to identify the skills that our students need to stand out and deliver something that can't be matched by their automated counterparts. There are a variety of skill sets that students — and people in general — need in order to prepare for whatever comes next in life. According to a 2019 study by *Forbes*,[2] the ten most vital skills necessary for the future of work are

1. Creativity
2. Emotional intelligence
3. Analytical thinking
4. Active learning with a growth mind-set
5. Judgment and decision making
6. Interpersonal communication skills
7. Leadership skills
8. Diversity and cultural intelligence
9. Technology skills
10. The ability to embrace change

Recognizing that most if not all of these skills fall outside of the mandated state/national learning standards that drive content-based instruction, one must consider that it is the pedagogy, or delivery of instruction, that will hone these vital skill sets. With that in mind, educators must consider shifting their instructional approaches so that students are exposed to situations and scenarios that force them to access, utilize, reflect upon, and hone these skills. Enter emergent technology.

There are many opportunities, some discussed through the stories in the pages of this book, and many others in the hearts and minds of educators around the globe, where emergent technology has contributed to the development of the skills identified by *Forbes* for the future of work. For example, what better way to foster empathy for victims of social injustice than the Becoming Homeless experience put out by Stanford. In Steven Sato's story about it in this book students were tasked with immersively assuming the identity of a homeless person whose story left a tremendous emotional impact on the user. One can argue that surely those students had their emotional intelligences tested and reflectively incurred growth as a result of that experience. In Matt Gottilla's story about designing a sustainable community in Google Blocks, students were tasked with accessing their leadership and communication skills to collectively create a final product. They employed both analytical-thinking and decision-making processes along with technology skills. This project alone touches upon almost all of the ten vital skills for the future — none of which were directly delivered as a result of mandated content through state or national standards but rather through innovative pedagogy supported by the adoption of emergent technology. If we continue, as educators, to consider how the technologies surrounding AR and VR afford us opportunities to expose students to a learning that extends far beyond their classrooms and communities, then we will revolutionize education with regard to learning experiences. Lessons that were once taught entirely in theory can now be practical, applied, and immersive, leading to more informed, experienced, and productive graduates entering the world beyond education.

The Future of Work: Hard Skills

Steve Isaacs's story spoke about exposing students to platforms like Unity to allow them to become creators of content and emphasizing the importance of providing them with skills that set them apart from the rest of the crowd. Steve's students had the incredible opportunity to acquire field experience working collaboratively with VR developers.

Through an ongoing relationship with hardware-provider ByteSpeed, Steve was introduced to Xennial Digital. Xennial Digital was seeking to work directly with students to develop VR content for schools. They were looking to bring students from a few schools together to collaborate with each other and developers in order to research and contribute directly to creating content. This was right in line with Steve's mission to have students create content for VR. Furthermore, it provided an opportunity for students to work directly with industry professionals, something Steve had been trying to facilitate. Recognizing the value in this opportunity, Steve reached out to some former students who were then in high school and let them know of this opportunity. Working collaboratively with middle-school students from Borough School in Morris Plains, New Jersey, the students were eager to learn from the experts in the field. They had the opportunity to suggest additions to existing content and to develop actual content in Unity with the support of the developers. The students used industry-standard software with professional mentors and acquired skills that will benefit them tremendously in the future.

As we continue to seek opportunities for students to learn through hands-on experiences, we must be reminded of the power that emergent technology has in providing these experiences. While some may see this technology as a privilege that is only afforded to the wealthiest of school communities, it is actually a technology that can level the playing field, affording all students the same learning opportunities by transporting students to the learning. Whether they are in a village in Guatemala, an island in the South Pacific, or a skyscraper in New York City, all students, with the technology in hand, have the same learning opportunities.

The XR Framework:
The Map to Future of Work

In every aspect of life there are skills and goals that serve a necessary purpose. Sometimes, we must take a moment to observe what is happening around us, assess the circumstances, and proceed with action based upon our analysis. These life moments can be defined as Absorb: we are absorbing what is happening in an effort to define this particular moment in our life. When students Absorb in their learning, through AR and VR, they are honing their skills of observation and evaluation in preparation for the future when these very skills are necessary for success.

Similarly, there are times in life that are defined by the actions we take within the parameters that are provided to us. These particular moments fall into the concept of Blend. When we are in a situation that requires us to use what is available or presented to us and we manipulate the moment to provide for a desired outcome, we are Blending our reality. This skill is critical for students moving into the workforce, where they will need to take what is available to them and adapt accordingly in an effort to increase productivity.

Lastly, there are those critically defining moments in life where we are required to design something new in order to proceed in a meaningful way. These moments demand that we think outside of the box, that we test our ability to produce unique and individual thoughts. These are the moments where we Create. Through the Create experiences that we provide to students in AR and VR, we are teaching them to think in ways that extend far beyond just what is in front of them and to become producers of solutions.

All three aspects of the XR Framework are equally critical to the adoption of emergent technology, and not one in particular rises above the others in regard to importance. They are not levels of adoption; rather, they describe the breadth of adoption. As educators, when we can provide students with learning experiences that encompass all three (Absorb, Blend, and Create), we are guiding students in accessing and building skills that they will apply to life situations. Just as with classroom practice, we must foster future decision makers who are empowered to absorb their surroundings when appropriate, blend to manipulate for a more desired outcome, and create solutions where none yet exist. AR and VR are the pathways to providing students with these necessary skills to be productive and purposeful future global citizens.

Experiencing Their Future

When Lilia, Christine's daughter, had her first experience in VR, she was seven years old. She went to work with her mother on Take Our Daughters and Sons to Work Day, a most coveted day for all children whose parents have a "cool job." After spending the day walking around the school buildings and checking in on the technology, Christine took Lilia down to the brand new STEAM learning lab in the upper-grade-level school. After proposing a few options, Lilia chose to experience the underwater ecosystems of the ocean on theBlu VR experience. Donning the HTC Vive headset, Lilia began her underwater adventure embraced by the marine animals that swam alongside her and entertained by the sea life who danced with her. Lilia looked around with complete awe as she took in the incredible immersive experience. With a giant grin on her face, she took the headset off, turned to her mother, and said with sheer joy in her voice, "Mom, this is amazing, I want to work with sea animals when I grow up."

Since that day, Lilia has taken a serious interest in reading as much non-fiction about marine life as she can find, watches TV shows that educate her about the ocean ecosystems, and continuously expresses interest in learning more about marine biology. Never would Lilia have had the opportunity to swim among the fish without the experiences afforded to her through virtual reality. Perhaps, this moment of awe will inspire her future career path in the same way that we can harness the power of AR and VR to inspire the future of all learners.

Continuing the Journey with Ready Learner One

We hope that you've enjoyed your journey through *Reality Bytes*. Now that you've finished, you may be wondering where to go next. A great starting point is to check out the Ready Learner One website at http://readylearner.one, where you can communicate online with other educators about AR and VR in the classroom, find out more information about all of the contributors to this book, and learn about all of the latest and greatest developments in the XR space for education. Just remember, as you embark on your own XR journey, you are not alone!

Acknowledgments

This book would not have been possible without the support and encouragement of Dave and Shelley Burgess. The development and design team of Lindsey Alexander and Sal Borriello from the Reading List helped us articulate our vision for the book in a way we could never have done alone. Our illustrator Manuel S. Herrera and cover designer Chad Beckerman were able to create images that perfectly captured what we envisioned in our heads.

Our partnership with Xennial Digital is a testament to the power of collaboration between the education and corporate spaces. Lorenzo Vallone and his team, including Aura Franco and Diego Silva, were fantastic to work with and very quickly supported our enthusiasm and ideas for the book by creating, modifying, and generating both VR and AR images that truly made our book more than a read — they helped make it an experience.

The efforts of Anna Hanson, Grant Hagen, and the team at ByteSpeed to champion our work have been greatly appreciated. Their commitment to providing customers with an amazing support structure was echoed in their feedback on our efforts.

Many companies supported our vision for the book by allowing us to use images of their products that supported you, the reader, in conceptualizing the tools. We would like to thank QuiverVision, MERGE, and Panoform for their contributions.

Lastly, we want to extend a thank you to our Ready Learner One family, who contributed their stories and insights to *Reality Bytes*: Amanda Fox, Amber Klebanoff, Ben Kelly, Bobby Carlton, Brian Cauthers, Brian Costello, Cherie Herring, David Saunders, Eugene Belyaev, George Barcenas, James McCrary, Jamie Donally, Dr. Jen Williams, John Dalgety, Kevin Chaja, Lorenzo Vallone, Matt Gottilla, Monica Arés, Sam Jang, Shannon Putman, Steve Bambury, Steve Isaacs, Steven Sato, Silvia Scuracchio, Suzanna Katz, Tisha Richmond, and Josh Williams.

Chapter Source Notes

Introduction

1 Augmented Reality for Enterprise Alliance, "Augmented Reality Defined," http://thearea.org/augmented-reality-defined/.

2 Daniel Freeman et al., "Virtual Reality in the Assessment, Understanding, and Treatment of Mental Health Disorders," *Psychological Medicine* 47, no. 14 (2017), 2393–400, https://www.ncbi.nlm.nih.gov/pubmed/28325167.

3 Matt Dunleavy, Chris Dede, and Rebecca Mitchell, "Affordances and Limitations of Immersive Participatory Augmented Reality Simulations for Teaching and Learning," *Journal of Science Eductaion and Technology*, 18, no. 1 (2009), 7–22. https://doi.org/10.1007/s10956-008-9119-1.

4 J. P. Gownder et al., "How Enterprise Smart Glasses Will Drive Workforce Enablement: Forecast: US Enterprise Adoption and Usage Of Smart Glasses," Forrester, report, April 21, 2016.

5 Murat Akçay and Gökçe Akçay, "Advantages and Challenges Associated with Augmented Reality for Education: A Systematic Review of the Literature," *Educational Research Review* 20 (2017), 1–11.

Chapter 1

1 University of Maryland Colloge of Computer, Mathematical, and Natural Sciences, "People Recall Information Better through Virtual Reality, Says New UMD Study," June 13, 2018, https://cmns.umd.edu/news-events/features/4155; Sol Rogers, "Virtual Reality: THE Learning Aid of The 21st Century," *Forbes*, March 15, 2019, https://www.forbes.com/sites/solrogers/2019/03/15/virtual-reality-the-learning-aid-of-the-21st-century/.

2 Bernard Blin, "The First Half Century (1895–1945): Milestones in Radio," *Unesco Courier*, February 1997, 2, 16.

3 Larry Cuban, *Teachers and Machines: The Classroom Use of Technology since 1920* (New York: Teachers College Press, 1986).

4 Harsh Vardhan, "Radio Broadcast Technology," *Resonance* 7, no. 1 (January 2002), 53–63.

5 Harsh Vardhan, "Radio Broadcast Technology," *Resonance* 7, no. 1 (January 2002), 53–63.

6 A. J. Romiszowsk, *The Selection and Use of Instructional Media* (London: Kogan Page Limited, 1974).

7 Sally D. Berman, "The Return of Educational Radio?" International Review of Research in Open and Distance Learning 9, no. 2, 1–8.

8 Sally D. Berman, "The Return of Educational Radio?" International Review of Research in Open and Distance Learning 9, no. 2, 1–8.

9 Jamesine Friend, "Interactive Radio Instruction: Developing Instructional Methods," *British Journal of Educational Technology* 20, no. 2 (1989), 106–114, http:/onlinelibrary.wiley.com/doi/10.1111/j.1467-8535.1989.tb00270.x/full.

10 Alfonso Gumucio Dagron, *Making Waves: Stories of Participatory Communication for Social Change: A Report to the Rockefeller Foundation* (New York: The Rockefeller Foundation, 2001), https://community. icann.org/download/attachments/58727397/Making%20Waves%20-%20 Stories%20for%20Participatory%20Communication%20-%20Alfonso%20 Gumucio%20Dagron%20for%20the%20Rockefeller%20Foundation. pdf?version=1&modificationDate=1464983918000&api=v2.

11 Scott D. Johnson and Steven R. Aragon, "An Instructional Strategy Framework for Online Learning Environments," *New Directions for Adult and Continuing Education* 2003, no. 100, 31–43, https://doi.org/10.1002/ace.117.

12 Ronald Phipps and Jamie Merisotis, "What's the Difference? A Review of Contemporary Research on the Effectiveness of Distance Learning in Higher Education," Institute or Higher Education Policy, April 1999, http://www. ihep.org/research/publications/whats-difference-review-contemporary-re-search-effectiveness-distance-learning.

13 Wilbur Lang Schramm, *Big Media, Little Media: Tools and Technologies for Instruction* (Beverly Hills, CA: Sage Publications, 1977).

14 Chris Dede, "The Evolution of Distance Education: Emerging Technologies and Distributed Learning," *American Journal of Distance Education*, 10, no. 2 (1996).

15 Lena Ballone Duran and Emilio Duran, "The 5E Instructional Model: A Learning Cycle Approach for Inquiry-Based Science Teaching," *Science Eductation Review* 3, no. 2 (2004), https://files.eric.ed.gov/fulltext/ EJ1058007.pdf.

16 National Education Association, "Preparing 21st Century Students for a Global Society," http://www.nea.org/assets/docs/A-Guide-to-Four-Cs.pdf.

17 International Society for Technology in Education, "ISTE Standards for Students," https://www.iste.org/standards/for-students.

18 International Society for Technology in Education, "ISTE Standards for Educators," https://www.iste.org/standards/for-educators.

19 Ruben R. Puentedura, "SAMR: A Brief Introduction," Hippasus, accessed November 6, 2019, http://hippasus.com/rrpweblog/archives/2015/10/SAMR_ABriefIntro.pdf

20 Micah Shippee, "Helping Others Along: Motivation Theory and the SAMR Model," blog post, October 4, 2018, https://micahshippee.com/2018/10/04/helping-others-along-motivation-theory-and-the-samr-model/.

Chapter 2

1 Texas Instruments, "DLP Automotive Chipset—Head-up Display," TI.com, http://www.ti.com/dlp-chip/automotive/applications/head-up-display-hud.html.

2 Chelsea Stark, "The Long and Winding Road to Personal Heads-Up Displays," Mashable, February 26, 2012, https://mashable.com/2012/02/26/heads-up-displays/.

Chapter 3

1 Michail Mantzios and Kyriaki Giannou, "When Did Coloring Books Become Mindful? Exploring the Effectiveness of a Novel Method of Mindfulness-Guided Instructions for Coloring Books to Increase Mindfulness and Decrease Anxiety," *Frontiers in Psychology* 9, no. 56 (2018), doi:10.3389/fpsyg.2018.00056; Priscilla Frank, "Why Coloring Could Be the New Alternative to Meditation," HuffPost, July 28, 2015, https://www.huffpost.com/entry/coloring-benefits-meditation_n_55b7c9c1e4b0074ba5a6724f; Joy Millam, "High School Library Coloring Center De-Stresses Students," School Library Journal, December 15, 2016, https://www.slj.com?detailStory=high-school-library-coloring-center-de-stresses-students.

2 DAQRI, "Essential Tools for the Digital Workforce," https://vimeo.com/264700740.

3 Literacy Planet, "How Physial Activity Affects School Performance," https://www.literacyplanet.com/au/legends/content/how-physical-activity-affects-school-performance/.

Chapter 4

1 Claire F. Deloria, *Liverpool Cemetery: A Walking Tour* (Syracuse, NY: Eagle Media, 1995).

Chapter 5

1 Daniel J. Boorstin, *The Discoverers* (New York: Vintage Books, 1985).

2 Rebekah Tuchscherer, "Walmart Uses Virtual Reality to Hire New Managers," *USA Today*, July 8, 2019, https://www.usatoday.com/story/tech/2019/07/08/walmart-uses-virtual-reality-hire-new-managers/1635311001/.

3 Stanford University, "Becoming Homeless: A Human Experience," Virtual Human Interaction Lab, https://vhil.stanford.edu/becominghomeless/.

Chapter 8

1 Elliot Hu-Au, "Xennial Digital's XDVR Portal: Playing with Science in VR," Virtual Reality for Education, November 7, 2018, http://virtualrealityforeducation.com/xennial-digitals-xdvr-learning-portal-playing-with-science-in-vr/.

2 Lubos Janoska, "What Really Is the Cone of Experience?" eLearning Industry, August, 28, 2017, https://elearningindustry.com/cone-of-experience-what-really-is.

Chapter 9

1 Damian Radcliffe, "Driverless Air Taxis, Drones, Pods: Dubai Puts Future Tech at Heart of Transportation," ZDNet, January 23, 2019, https://www.zdnet.com/article/driverless-air-taxis-drones-pods-dubai-puts-future-tech-at-heart-of-transportation/.

2 Bernard Marr, "The 10 Vital Skills You Will Need for the Future of Work," *Forbes*, April 29, 2019, https://www.forbes.com/sites/bernardmarr/2019/04/29/the-10-vital-skills-you-will-need-for-the-future-of-work/#2a831bf73f5b.

About the Authors

Christine Lion-Bailey

Christine Lion-Bailey is the chief strategy officer of Ready Learner One. She also serves as an elementary principal and director of technology and innovation for a New Jersey school district. Christine is an adjunct professor of education technology at Ramapo College of New Jersey and is a Google for Education Certified Innovator and BrainPop Certified Educator. She presents, delivers keynotes, and leads workshops at many conferences on various innovation topics, both nationally and internationally. She also consults with school districts to support innovative educational practices. Christine is an advocate for innovative thought and practices in schools, both through instruction and leadership.

Jesse Lubinsky

Jesse Lubinsky is the chief learning officer of Ready Learner One. Prior to entering the field of education, he was a technology consultant for Fortune 500 companies. His work has been published in the book *High-Tech Teaching Success!* by Prufrock Press. As a director of technology and innovation and chief information officer, he received a Technology Leader Pioneer Award from the Lower Hudson Regional Information Center. Jesse is a Google for Education Certified Innovator and Trainer, a CoSN Certified Education Technology Leader, an adjunct professor of education technology at Pace University, a member of the Google Earth Education Experts team, and a frequent keynote speaker and presenter who has recently given educational technology presentations across North America, Europe, Asia, the Middle East, and Australia. Jesse is also cohost of the Partial Credit podcast.

Micah Shippee, PhD

Micah Shippee, PhD, is the chief executive officer of Ready Learner One and author of *WanderlustEDU: A Guide to Innovation, Change, and Adventure*. Micah is a social-studies teacher and educational-technology trainer with two decades of experience. He serves the education community in several capacities, including as the eastern US lead for the Google Earth Education Experts team, as a Google for Education Certified Innovator, and as a National Geographic Educator. Micah is listed by EdTech Digest as one of the one hundred top influencers in education technology for 2019–2020. Micah's innovative approach to education finds him working to bridge the gap between research and practice. As an author, educational consultant, and keynote speaker, he focuses on the adoption of innovation through the development of learning cultures that embrace change. Micah believes that innovativeness is the pedagogy of the future.

About Ready Learner One

Ready Learner One provides innovative solutions for learning and specializes in working with emergent technologies. Founded by passionate, experienced educators who recognize the power that technology and innovative practices have to shift learning practices and outcomes, Ready Learner One offers a vast array of learning solutions. You can find out more about us at http://readylearner.one.

About Our Partners

The Xennial Digital Team

Xennial Digital is an award-winning XR software development company with offices in Miami, New York, and Bogotá that specializes in:

- Production of advanced XR experiences for education, training, sales enablement, and other enterprise areas
- Virtual telepresence solutions to enable multiple people to interact within the same virtual space/environment
- VR solutions/platforms for high-end devices (HTC Vive, Oculus) through low-end VR devices (Google Cardboard)
- AR solutions for mobile applications (smartphones and tablets)
- Mixed-reality solutions for Magic Leap and Microsoft HoloLens platforms

Xennial Digital is the developer of XD Learning, an advanced XR-based learning platform designed to measure and optimize learner performance for K–12, higher education, and corporate training.

Xennial Digital's team is proud to have contributed content, chapter imagery, and AR content for this book. Download XD Learning for free or learn more about Xennial Digital at www.xennialdigital.com.

Lorenzo Vallone

Lorenzo is cofounder and CTO of Xennial Digital. He is a dreamer and a doer, an entrepreneur with a passion for education, the environment, digital marketing, and technology.

Aura Franco

Aura is a senior account director at Xennial Digital helping clients create VR and AR solutions. She is a connector, and with her infectious kindness and encouragement, she helps bring people together to do their best work.

Diego Silva

Diego is the XR digital director at Xennial Digital. He is a creative visionary with 3-D-design and XR-technology expertise.

About 8th Wall

Founded in 2016, 8th Wall is a computer vision software company that makes it possible for anyone to build interactive AR experiences that run on all mobile devices. Breaking down walls between the digital and physical worlds, 8th Wall allows creators and brands to develop immersive content that can be instantly published to the mobile web. It has powered AR activations for brands across industry verticals including retail, food and beverage, travel and tourism, automotive, fashion, sports, and entertainment. Notable customers of the platform include Sony Pictures, Miller Lite, British Gas, Heineken, Swiss Airlines, Toyota, EVA Air, Porsche, Red Bull, *Time* magazine, Adidas, COACH, and LEGO.

WWW.MANUELDRAWS.COM

The Illustrator
Manuel S. Herrera

Manuel is an educator, an international speaker, and an illustrator. He currently serves as the innovation coordinator for the Affton school district located in a suburb of St. Louis. He is an adjunct professor at Webster University, teaching digital video for educators and the design of ed tech facilities. In addition to these roles, Manuel is the communications and design lead for Connected Learning, an educational nonprofit located in St. Louis. Manuel has keynoted, presented, and led workshops at educational conferences like SXSW EDU, ISTE, TCEA, MassCUE, FETC, and .EDU. He specializes in sketchnoting, visual thinking, design thinking, and 3-D printing and design. In 2018 Manuel became a Google Innovator at LAX18, and in 2016 he was named the Midwest Education Technology Conference Spotlight Educator. You can follow Manuel on Twitter and Instagram at @manuelherrera33.

More from
DAVE BURGESS
Consulting, inc.

Since 2012, DBCI has been publishing books that inspire and equip educators to be their best. For more information on our DBCI titles or to purchase bulk orders for your school, district, or book study, visit **DaveBurgessconsulting. com/DBCIbooks**.

More from Ready Learner One

WanderlustEDU by Micah Shippee, PhD

Like a PIRATE™ Series

Teach Like a PIRATE by Dave Burgess

eXPlore Like a Pirate by Michael Matera

Learn Like a Pirate by Paul Solarz

Play Like a Pirate by Quinn Rollins

Run Like a Pirate by Adam Welcome

Lead Like a PIRATE™ Series

Lead Like a PIRATE by Shelley Burgess and Beth Houf

Balance Like a Pirate by Jessica Cabeen, Jessica Johnson, and Sarah Johnson

Lead beyond Your Title by Nili Bartley

Lead with Culture by Jay Billy

Lead with Literacy by Mandy Ellis

Leadership & School Culture

Culturize by Jimmy Casas

Escaping the School Leader's Dunk Tank by Rebecca Coda and Rick Jetter

From Teacher to Leader by Starr Sackstein

The Innovator's Mindset by George Couros

Kids Deserve It! by Todd Nesloney and Adam Welcome

Let Them Speak by Rebecca Coda and Rick Jetter

The Limitless School by Abe Hege and Adam Dovico

The Pepper Effect by Sean Gaillard

The Principled Principal by Jeffrey Zoul and Anthony McConnell

Relentless by Hamish Brewer

The Secret Solution by Todd Whitaker, Sam Miller, and Ryan Donlan

Start. Right. Now. by Todd Whitaker, Jeffrey Zoul, and Jimmy Casas

Stop. Right. Now. by Jimmy Casas and Jeffrey Zoul

They Call Me "Mr. De" by Frank DeAngelis

Unmapped Potential by Julie Hasson and Missy Lennard

Word Shift by Joy Kirr

Your School Rocks by Ryan McLane and Eric Lowe

Technology & Tools

50 Things You Can Do with Google Classroom by Alice Keeler and Libbi Miller

50 Things to Go Further with Google Classroom by Alice Keeler and Libbi Miller

140 Twitter Tips for Educators by Brad Currie, Billy Krakower, and Scott Rocco

Block Breaker by Brian Aspinall

Code Breaker by Brian Aspinall

Google Apps for Littles by Christine Pinto and Alice Keeler

Master the Media by Julie Smith

Shake Up Learning by Kasey Bell

Social LEADia by Jennifer Casa-Todd

Teaching Math with Google Apps by Alice Keeler and Diana Herrington

Teachingland by Amanda Fox and Mary Ellen Weeks

Teaching Methods & Materials

All 4s and 5s by Andrew Sharos

The Classroom Chef by John Stevens and Matt Vaudrey

Ditch That Homework by Matt Miller and Alice Keeler

Ditch That Textbook by Matt Miller

Don't Ditch That Tech by Matt Miller, Nate Ridgway, and Angelia Ridgway

EDrenaline Rush by John Meehan

Educated by Design by Michael Cohen, The Tech Rabbi

The EduProtocol Field Guide by Marlena Hebern and Jon Corippo

The EduProtocol Field Guide: Book 2 by Marlena Hebern and Jon Corippo

Instant Relevance by Denis Sheeran

LAUNCH by John Spencer and A.J. Juliani

Make Learning MAGICAL by Tisha Richmond

Pure Genius by Don Wettrick

The Revolution by Darren Ellwein and Derek McCoy

Shift This! by Joy Kirr

Spark Learning by Ramsey Musallam

Sparks in the Dark by Travis Crowder and Todd Nesloney

Table Talk Math by John Stevens

The Wild Card by Hope and Wade King

The Writing on the Classroom Wall by Steve Wyborney

Inspiration, Professional Growth & Personal Development

Be REAL by Tara Martin

Be the One for Kids by Ryan Sheehy

Creatively Productive by Lisa Johnson

The EduNinja Mindset by Jennifer Burdis

Empower Our Girls by Lynmara Colón and Adam Welcome

The Four O'Clock Faculty by Rich Czyz

How Much Water Do We Have? by Pete and Kris Nunweiler

P Is for Pirate by Dave and Shelley Burgess

A Passion for Kindness by Tamara Letter

The Path to Serendipity by Allyson Apsey

Sanctuaries by Dan Tricarico

Shattering the Perfect Teacher Myth by Aaron Hogan

Stories from Webb by Todd Nesloney

Talk to Me by Kim Bearden

Teach Me, Teacher by Jacob Chastain

TeamMakers by Laura Robb and Evan Robb

Through the Lens of Serendipity by Allyson Apsey

The Zen Teacher by Dan Tricarico

Children's Books

Beyond Us by Aaron Polansky

Cannonball In by Tara Martin

Dolphins in Trees by Aaron Polansky

I Want to Be a Lot by Ashley Savage

The Princes of Serendip by Allyson Apsey

Zom-Be a Design Thinker by Amanda Fox